n of George 1.   By H. Overton and J. Hoole.

KENSINGTON PALACE

By the same author

A POET IN PARLIAMENT: *Life of W. M. Praed*

THOMAS BARNES OF 'THE TIMES'

BRITISH JOURNALISTS AND NEWSPAPERS

NORMAN O'NEILL: *A Life of Music*

CHARLES KEENE

MARTIN TUPPER: *His Rise and Fall*

JAMES PRYDE

LEWIS CARROLL

THE ROYAL SOCIETY OF ARTS, *1754–1954* (*With Kenneth W. Luckhurst*)

SIR JOSHUA REYNOLDS

ARTHUR RACKHAM: *His Life and Work*

THE FORGOTTEN KING AND OTHER ESSAYS

WRITING BETWEEN THE LINES (*autobiography*)

HOLLAND HOUSE IN KENSINGTON

TALKS WITH FUDDY AND OTHER PAPERS, *etc. etc.*

Kensington Palace, South Front.
Detail from watercolour by W. Westall, 1819.

KENSINGTON PALACE

BY DEREK HUDSON

PETER DAVIES : LONDON

© 1968 by Derek Hudson
First Published 1968
432 06951 8

Printed in Great Britain by
Cox & Wyman Ltd, London, Fakenham and Reading

CONTENTS

ILLUSTRATIONS

For Rob and Barbara

AUTHOR'S PREFACE

I am grateful to Her Majesty the Queen for her gracious permission to make use of material in the Royal Library and Archives, Windsor Castle, to reproduce works of art from the Royal collection, and to visit unoccupied private apartments at Kensington Palace. I am also grateful to Her Royal Highness Princess Marina, Duchess of Kent, for permission to publish a photograph of the staircase in her apartment there. And I wish to thank Mr Robert Mackworth-Young, Librarian, Windsor Castle, and his staff for their kind assistance in my researches, and Major Rennie Maudslay, Assistant Keeper of the Privy Purse, for his courteous advice. I am greatly indebted to Mr John Charlton, of the Ministry of Public Building and Works, for sharing his expert knowledge of the Palace with me and for showing me parts of the Palace not open to the public; and to Mr H. G. Yexley, Architect of the Historic Buildings Section of the Ministry, for allowing me to draw on a most interesting unpublished paper of his on its history. I also wish to express my gratitude to Sir Philip Hay for his friendly encouragement and hospitality; and to Mrs Sally Kington, Librarian of the London Museum, and Miss D. A. Fennemore for some extremely helpful assistance and research.

This is the first time that the history of Kensington Palace has been written at length, but I should express my obligation to Thomas Faulkner's *History and Antiquities of Kensington* (1820), and to monographs on the Palace by W. J. Loftie (1898) and Ernest Law (1899). I have been particularly indebted to two learned articles by Mr Patrick A. Faulkner (one of them written in collaboration with Mr G. H. Chettle), and to Vol. VII of the Wren Society edited by Mr Arthur T. Bolton and Mr H. Duncan Hendry. Lady Longford's excellent biography *Victoria R.I.* has been an invaluable source of instruction; and I have been obliged to her for answering my queries on certain points. Many other writers whose work has aided me are listed, with their books and articles, in the bibliography; I have included references in the text to material in the Royal Archives (R.A.) and the Public Record Office (P.R.O.). Other helpers whom I remember gratefully are Mr Oliver Millar, Mrs Jane Bartlett, Mr W. E. Boardman, the staffs of the Kensington Central Library and the London Library, and a member of the A.R.P. Department of the Kensington Borough Council.

I have to thank Messrs Evans Brothers for permission to publish an extract from *For My Grandchildren* by H.R.H. Princess Alice.

For assistance in obtaining the illustrations, I am indebted to the Librarian, Windsor Castle; the National Portrait Gallery; Magdalene College, Cambridge; the Ministry of Public Building and Works, and its Photographic Librarian, Mrs M. P. Harper; the Marquess of Hertford; the Marquess of Bristol; Sir John Summerson; and Mrs Barbara Edwards. The sources of illustrations are named in the list on pp. vii–ix, and I should like to express my obligation to all concerned in making them available.   D.H.

Kensington, January, 1968.

INTRODUCTION

The traveller journeying westward from Hyde Park Corner is first aware of Kensington Palace as a group of red brick buildings to the north of the road, separated from the railings by the grass slopes of Kensington Gardens. The south front, with its ornamental vases over the central windows, confers an impression of dignity and formal austerity; as the eye runs westward along the range of less pretentious domestic buildings, the Palace appears also a homely place to be lived in. It has always lacked the fanciful attraction of its neighbour Holland House; but, unlike that delightful mansion, has the great advantage of still standing intact.

Beside the Royal Garden Hotel a gateway marked 'Private Road' leads directly to the entrance portico. The gate pillars are surmounted by the arms of England and by an escutcheon-of-pretence for Orange, immediate reminders that William III was the Palace's first royal occupant. But, passing this gateway, and averting our eyes from the discordant modern hotel, we shall best approach the Palace and understand its situation by taking the next turning to the north into Kensington Palace Gardens, a broad avenue lined by imposing Victorian mansions which are largely occupied by foreign embassies. This soon brings us to Palace Green, once known as 'The Moor' and used as a parade ground in the eighteenth century. Here several curious ancient buildings, including a conduit and a water tower, have long since vanished; but on the right are the old cavalry barracks, now converted into apartments occupied by the Queen's staff; and on the left is the unremarkable house designed by Thackeray, in which he died in 1863. Thackeray was fully conscious of the historical associations of the Palace, which he introduced into *The Virginians*;

indeed the Palace has been a good deal written up in the picturesque flowery manner both by him and by Leigh Hunt.

Let us take a walk around the Palace, and get a preliminary view of the State Apartments as they stand today. Halted in front of the portico, we find that we cannot advance to the left or enter Clock Court through the archway, for this southern part of the Palace is appropriated to the residences of Princess Marina and Princess Margaret, and the police are about. To reach the public entrance to the State Apartments, we must enter Kensington Gardens by the adjacent gate on the right, and walk round the Palace, twice turning to the left. In doing so, we suspect that the Broad Walk is rather too broad, the Round Pond rather too magnificent, both having been made to accord with George I's grandiose ambitions for the modest Wren palace he had inherited. Passing Queen Victoria's statue, the air may strike cool – is it true, perhaps, that the pond brought a certain misty dampness to the Palace, as some later inhabitants have believed?

The Wren doorway (facing east) by which we enter the State Apartments (see the plan on p. 134) shows the royal monogram of William and Mary; this range of buildings contains three storeys above a basement, and a panelled staircase with a blue carpet leads to Queen Mary's Gallery on the first floor, which looks eastward over Kensington Gardens. Here the dark oak panelling has been restored to what it was in Queen Mary's day. The fireplace overmantels also date from 1690; the Queen's elaborate writing cabinet stands against the south wall. It is a pleasant room: its length (84 feet) makes it large enough for a ball, but the relatively narrow width diminishes its grandeur, allowing for comfort and accessibility on more ordinary occasions.

The next three rooms in sequence are perhaps the most intimate and domestic in the whole Palace. They are the Queen's Closet, Private Dining-room, and Queen's Drawing

Room, small, unpretentious, typical of the country house of their period. Queen Mary and Queen Anne lived in these rooms, and it was in one of them that Anne gave her last interview to the Duchess of Marlborough. The rooms, all facing east, are dark, but they suggest snug comfort rather than gloom, confirming Leigh Hunt's impression: 'Windsor Castle is a place to receive monarchs in; Buckingham Palace to see fashion in; Kensington Palace seems a place to drink tea in. . . .'

The succession of four rooms that follows and runs at right angles to the previous set is quite different. Replacing the more modest rooms of the original building, Nottingham House, they represent George I's idea of what a palace ought to be. One could still drink tea in them, but there is more space to strike superior attitudes. Most of them have elaborate ceilings painted by William Kent. The one that we enter first is the Privy Chamber. Facing west, its windows afford a good view of the interior of Clock Court and of the doorways of its private residences. We pass into the Cupola Room (or Cube Room): a piece of magnificence intended to *épater le bourgeois,* more opulent than lovable. The King's Drawing Room has a little more grace, and benefits from the view over the Round Pond. To the north is the Council Chamber; and behind its west wall is a staircase, which we do not see unless we are very inquisitive.

The next three rooms, leading to the south-east corner, furnished and decorated in the early Victorian style, are on a smaller scale. First, there is the royal bedroom, in which Queen Victoria was sleeping when she learned of her accession to the throne; then an ante-room; then the Nursery. The two last rooms may have been used as dressing-rooms by William III and the first two Georges. A doorway in the ante-room leads to another set of back-stairs; Queen Victoria went down them to her first Council.

We come next to the King's Gallery of 1695, running along the south front, 96 feet long and the finest room in the Palace, with its wind-dial, fine cornice and carvings, and one of Kent's most ambitious ceilings. A passage at the west end leads to the King's Grand Staircase, a transformation by George I of Wren's simple early stairs, the walls decorated by Kent as a *coup d'oeil*. The stairs are no longer functional, but we are anyway prevented from attempting a regal descent. We find ourselves next in the Presence Chamber; then go back to the open air by the way we came.

By walking a few yards outside along a pathway, we can, at present, visit the London Museum, and incidentally see the remaining principal rooms of the Palace on the two lower floors of the main block, that is to say the ground floor and semi-basement. These include the rooms in which Queen Victoria was born and in which she held her first Council, while to the west we come to the hall and double staircase designed as the chief entrance in the early nineteenth century.

These rooms are all that we can visit as members of the public. A large part of the Palace remains out of sight. If we are fortunately privileged, we may go on to explore the two arcaded courts to the north, Prince of Wales's Court and Princesses' Court, built by George I in the seventeen-twenties, which are consigned to offices and private apartments. They have some of the shady quiet and retired charm of Oxford college quadrangles. Princesses' Court to the east contains the house, earlier in date, built for the Maids of Honour; it is luckily well preserved. The western court has the handsome residence originally intended for George I's mistress, the Duchess of Kendal; photographs published in *Country Life* show how beautiful this was when it was occupied by the Countess Granville as recently as 1928; but since bombs fell on its roof in 1940, it has stood empty and derelict. The western range of the western court contains the chapel

xvi

formed in 1834, now divided by the insertion of a new floor.

Beyond these courts, to the north, are stable buildings, an attractive row of converted cottages, and of course Queen Anne's stately Orangery. The compactness of the Palace is best realised from a low-level aerial photograph, which gives the whole complex of buildings more symmetry than it seems to have from the ground. But if the photograph is taken from a still greater height, we get a remarkable impression of the Palace in its natural setting, at the head of the hundreds of acres of Kensington Gardens and Hyde Park (Plate XV). The Round Pond and the Serpentine now stand out as the vast sheets of water they are; the avenues radiating from the Pond emphasize the simplicity of the eighteenth-century landscape design; while away to the south-east, Green Park and St. James's Park are seen as continuing links in the chain of royal parks, hemmed in by bricks and mortar. Such a view well explains why William III bought Nottingham House in 1689, and why George V liked Kensington best of the London palaces.

In the pages that follow I have attempted to describe not only the considerable part that the Palace has played in the nation's affairs but also the changing fashions of royal domesticity over three hundred years. Inevitably, it must be a study of strength and weakness in high places, of loyalty and irresponsibility, though the former predominates. There are intrigue and asthma, melancholy, integrity, tragedy, eccentricity, lechery and wit. And the Palace cannot be separated in the account from the surrounding parkland of old Nottingham House, which as Kensington Gardens has for two centuries brought the Palace close to the knowledge and affections of all kinds of Londoners.

1 · HOUSE INTO PALACE

The eastern boundary of Kensington straggles illogically southwards from the Harrow Road, over the Bayswater Road, and along the Broad Walk of Kensington Gardens until it reaches the Kensington Road, when it turns to the east, goes half-way down Queen's Gate, and then sheers eastward again to join the Brompton Road. Until 1899 Kensington Palace was part of the parish of St Margaret's, Westminster; and, strictly, Kensington Gardens, the Albert Memorial and the Albert Hall still belong to Westminster – a distinction that is not recognized in practice. According to Thomas Faulkner, it is supposed that the anomaly arose 'before the bounds of parishes were definitively settled, and that the lands belonged to some opulent person whose residence was in Westminster, and which therefore in old assessments were rated in the parish where his capital mansion lay'. But W. J. Loftie's attempt to locate the ancient manor-house of the manor of Neyt on the site of Kensington Palace – and to trace its connection with royalty, in the person of John of Gaunt, back to the year 1381 – cannot be taken seriously; it is best disregarded.

The story of Kensington Palace, like that of neighbouring Holland House and Campden House, begins with a sheet in the book of drawings of John Thorpe, surveyor and architect, (c. 1563–1655) preserved at the Soane Museum (page 2). The drawing bears the inscription 'Sr. Geo: Coppin', and can be dated, at the earliest, to the year 1605, which is approximately the date of the Holland House drawing in the same collection. It is a significant document in the development of house planning, marking a phase in the transition from a medieval lay-out to that of the conventional eighteenth-century villa.

I

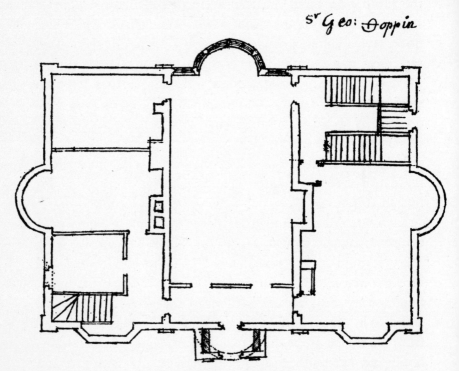

offices & Cellers under ground.

Sr Geo: Coppin

Drawing for Sir George Coppin's house, later Nottingham House, by
John Thorpe, *c.* 1605.

The drawing shows the principal floor, which had 'offices &
Cellers under ground' in a semi-basement. The entrance, on
the south side, faced the Kensington Road, with a flight of
steps leading up to the main porch. The hall, to which this
door gave admission, was still typically medieval; there were
screens at the south end and a dais at the north end; behind
the dais were a large bow window and side windows. On both
sides of the hall large rooms were planned, lit by bow windows: that on the west side (facing what is now Clock Court)
was probably a chapel; that on the east the parlour. The 'Great
stairs' were placed to the east of the dais; on the floor above
there may have been a 'great chamber' and a gallery; and over
this an attic floor.

Such was the rough plan, partly conjectural, of Sir George
Coppin's compact house, which was destined to survive for a
century, until it was completely rebuilt in about 1720 and
incorporated into the remodelled Palace. Sir George Coppin,
knighted in 1603, became a Clerk of the Crown to James I,
and died in 1619. He acquired the land for his house in 1604-5
from Sir Walter Cope, the great landowner of the neighbourhood and the builder of Holland House. As with Holland
House, it is difficult to say whether John Thorpe was actually
the architect of Sir George Coppin's house, or whether he
based his drawing on someone else's design. What is certain is
that Thorpe had a considerable practice among the officials
of King James's court, and was closely concerned not only
with the Coppin house at Kensington, but also with those
houses which Sir Baptist Hicks (Lord Campden) and Sir
Walter Cope erected farther to the west. Both Thorpe and
Coppin were liverymen of St Martin-in-the-Fields; many of
Thorpe's commissions derived from its parishioners. If the
Coppin house could be accepted as originating entirely from
Thorpe, his standing as a creative architect would be en-
hanced.

The estate that Sir George Coppin obtained from Sir Walter Cope seems to have comprised the greater part of the present grounds of Kensington Palace and Kensington Gardens. According to surveys of 1619 and 1631, it contained thirty-six acres of land; various further closes and messuages of unspecified extent, including a close called Thomas's Field; another 'parcel of land, called the Long Park Close', and other fields on the boundary of Hyde Park, to the extent of eleven acres.

In about 1620 the house passed into more distinguished ownership, when it was sold by Sir George Coppin's son Thomas to Sir Heneage Finch, who was appointed Recorder of London in 1621, and Speaker of the House of Commons in the first Parliament of Charles I. On Finch's death in 1631, his second son John, a boy of five, succeeded to the house; he became a physician, and spent much of his life abroad; at one time he held a professorship at Pisa, and later was appointed Minister to the Grand Duke of Tuscany and Ambassador at Constantinople. He sold the house in 1661 to his elder brother Heneage, an able lawyer who was made Solicitor-General and created a baronet on the Restoration in 1660.

Sir Heneage Finch is known to have been in occupation of the house in 1663, and lived there until his death in 1682. During these years he rose to the summit of his profession. His discretion in affairs and his learning as a constitutional lawyer made him indispensable to Crown and Parliament at a time when the constitution had to be re-established after the Cromwellian dictatorship. Attorney-General in 1670, Lord Keeper of the Seals in 1673, he became Lord Chancellor in 1674, and finally was created first Earl of Nottingham in 1681. Henceforth his house was known as Nottingham House.

We know little of the house at this period, except that

mention of an 'Old Brewhouse' and an 'Old Stable'* indicates that outbuildings were attached to it, apparently at the north-west angle. Sir Heneage set about improving the grounds. In 1663 Charles II granted him a piece of land, ten feet wide, to the east of the property, between his park and Hyde Park; the strip extended from 'the south highway, leading to the town of Kensington, and from thence crossing to the north highway, leading to the town of Acton'. Along this strip he constructed a ha-ha and planted an avenue of trees. The domestic gardens to the south of the mansion, with a fountain and summer-house, were already famous when Pepys visited them on 14 June 1664 – 'into Sir Heneage Finche's Garden and seeing the fountain, and singing there with the ladies, and a mighty fine cool place it is, with a great laver of water in the middle and the bravest place for music I ever heard'. Four years later, on another visit, Pepys mentions a grotto.

After the death of the first Earl of Nottingham in 1682, the house came into the possession of his son, Daniel Finch, the second Earl, who was then First Lord of the Admiralty. This Nottingham was dark as a Spaniard, a tall, thin, solemn person with a lugubrious expression. He was known as Don Diego and Don Dismal. Swift made fun of him. He became the leader of the new Tory party which held itself apart from the Jaco-bites; he was cautious about sponsoring William of Orange, but threw in his lot with the new régime after William had landed in November 1688. Both King William (Plate I) and Queen Mary (Plate I) learned to value him as a man of inte-grity. In December he was made one of the secretaries of state with charge of the War Department.

There is some evidence that by 1689 Nottingham House stood empty, in a poor state of repair. William III was looking

*This is not the building now occupied by Sir Alan and Lady Lascelles, to the north-west of the Palace block, facing southwards down the drive by Palace Green, which was erected c. 1740.

for a home near London in a situation more favourable to his health than Whitehall. He did not like being near the river, because this was bad for his asthma; moreover, Whitehall Palace was inconvenient – and he was supposed to dine in public there. Hampton Court did not provide a full answer; not only was it exposed to the river mists, but it was too far from London for his Ministers to be able conveniently to visit him. The King and Queen were deeply interested in Hampton Court, where the Master Surveyor of the Office of Works, Sir Christopher Wren, was soon busily employed, but as a compromise some half-way house seems to have been desirable. The King therefore made an excursion to Kensington, where he inspected Holland House, which he did not like, and Nottingham House, which he preferred. As a result, Narcissus Luttrell wrote in his diary on 18 June 1689: 'The King hath bought the Earl of Nottingham's house at Kensington for 18,000 guineas and designs it for his seat in the winter, being near Whitehall.'

The King's new country retreat was only a small house. It was at first called Kensington House, rather than Kensington Palace. Even after gradual enlargement to meet the needs of the court over forty years, it remained essentially domestic in character. Kensington Palace today has an informal charm deriving largely from its modest beginnings and architectural irregularity. If we expect to see a striking example of the art of Sir Christopher Wren, architect of the transformation, we shall be disappointed; he was denied the opportunity of imposing his overall conception from the outset, for King William – and equally Queen Mary – were in a hurry to leave Whitehall, and wished to see the existing Nottingham House enlarged as soon as possible. No doubt he would have been better pleased if he could have knocked down the old house and started again; but, remembering his difficulties, there is ample opportunity to admire the ingenuity with which he overcame them. Successful building in brick requires great artistry; as Coventry Patmore said, 'Sir Christopher Wren could not build a common brick house without impressing his own character upon it.'

The work of alteration and addition began without delay. On 3 July 1689 contracts were signed with John Hayward, Carpenter, and Thomas Hughes, Bricklayer. Wren's hurried procedure was risky; he ran up his new outer walls in brick, but formed the interior with trussed timber partitions, on which he balanced the chimney breasts and brick stacks. There was an early set-back, Narcissus Luttrell noting on 7 November 1689, that 'the additional buildings to the King's house at Kensington, being newly covered with lead, fell down on a sudden, and hurt several people and killed some, the Queen was herself there but little before'.

Queen Mary, who stayed at Holland House during the rebuilding, took the accident philosophically, saying that it 'shewed me plainly the hand of God was in it, and I was truly humbled'. Notwithstanding the mishap, the Court moved to Kensington for Christmas. John Evelyn's diary of 25 February 1690 records: 'I went to Kensington, which King William had bought of Lord Nottingham and altered, but was yet a patched building, but with the garden however it is a very sweet villa, having to it the Park and a straight new way through the Park.' The 'new way' is still partly to be seen in 'Rotten Row' (Route du Roi); it was provided with lamp posts on each side for the King's benefit, to combat those notorious Kensington dangers, fog and footpads.

At the corners of the old house, which had apparently survived more or less intact since its building in 1605, Wren added four new blocks or 'pavilions'. He skilfully contrived symmetrical elevations on the west, south, and east. The north side was irregular, perhaps because existing outbuildings had to be retained. An interesting drawing by Sutton Nicholls (title page), probably of 1689, indicates the effect of Wren's early alterations on the north side. It shows Thorpe's semi-circular bay carried up to the storey above, with stairs approaching a porch at ground level (which do not appear on Thorpe's plan).

The 'Kensington Pay Booke' for Wren's alterations of 1689–90 emphasizes that the house had to be considerably 'patched'. Thomas Hughes, the bricklayer, was paid for 'making good ye gable ends of ye Old House' and 'raising ye walls of ye gable ends and mending ye battlements and tyling of ye old House', also for 'finishing ye front of ye old House'.

The main entrance was planned on the west, where an arch-way, surmounted by a clock-tower and a weather-vane of the William and Mary monogram, gave on to a large courtyard, with two-storeyed wings attached to two of the new pavilions (Plate XIV). The north side of the courtyard accommodated the palace kitchens, and beyond them were two irregular courtyards enclosing kitchens and offices, called Green Cloth Court – from the offices of the Board of Green Cloth (the accounts committee of the royal household) which divided them – and Pump Court. On the south side of Clock Court was a corridor called the 'Stone Gallery', backed by rooms for the courtiers – access to the gallery being obtained from the west by a pleasant colonnaded portico facing Palace Green, 'with 8 pilasters of deals'. The two eastern pavilions were given over to the King's apartments; the north-west pavilion and the old Great Hall to those of the Queen. The south-west pavilion contained the King's staircase, as well as the chapel and guard-room. As always, Wren was overstrained, with

8

St Paul's a continual burden, and Hampton Court and many other commissions besides; yet the work advanced with such headlong speed that, despite the accident already mentioned, the King and Queen were in residence within six months.

The new Queen's Gallery, 84 feet in length, running northwards from the north-west pavilion, was erected in 1690–1. At the northern end of this gallery, Wren built a delightful staircase with oak balusters, which now provides entrance for the public who visit the State Apartments. Adjoining the staircase to the west was a pleasant set of panelled rooms on three floors, of about the same date, used by the Maids of Honour (now No. 10 Kensington Palace). The new gallery impaired the symmetry of Wren's original scheme, and a fire which destroyed the south side of Clock Court in 1691 suggested further alterations: the south-west pavilion was rebuilt as a great guard-chamber in two storeys (a finely decorated room which had gone by 1820), and the King's staircase was enlarged and became more imposing; in 1692 a portico (long since destroyed) was built between the two western pavilions.

Daniel Defoe's *Tour Thro' the Whole Island of Great Britain* has a paragraph about the fire of 1691:

'This South Wing was burnt down by Accident, the King and Queen being both there, the Queen was a little surprized at first, apprehending some Treason, but King *William* a Stranger to Fears smil'd at the Suggestion, chear'd Her Majesty up, and being soon dress'd, they both walked out into the Garden, and stood there some Hours till they perceived the Fire by the help that came in, and by the Diligence of the Foot Guards, was gotten under Foot.'

The Chapel Royal – perhaps a survival of the chapel of Nottingham House – remained after the enlargement of the great staircase. This chapel was sumptuously adorned; William Emmett received payment in April 1690 for carving '62 Ballisters in ye railes before ye Communion Table', '2 large Imperial Crowns over ye door', and '4 Spandrells of foliage and cyphers of their Majesties'. One must regret that the chapel was demolished in 1834, 'the Duchess of Kent requiring the space'; and a new chapel was then made out of a kitchen.

The 'Pay Bookes' for 1690–1 are meticulous in detailing the work carried out by an army of carpenters, joiners, masons, plasterers, bricklayers and plumbers. They extend to the lavatory arrangements, as the following entry shows: *'To Isaac Thompson*, Engine Maker, for making a forcing Engine to force ye Water into ye Cisternes by ye King's Kitchin & into ye Q's stoole. For making a Stoole for ye Queene, for making a Seate & covering it with Velvet, for a washer for ye Cistern and a ring in it in ye Stoole roome'. In December 1694 John Churchill, Carpenter, was 'making new Racks for ye King's Champaine wine and setting up shelves there', but before the next entry Queen Mary had died, on 28 December 1694, and Churchill is credited with 'mending ye steps of ye grt Stairs yt was broke in carrying ye Q's body down'.

The Queen's death at Kensington made William more than ever attached to the Palace. He lost interest in his idea of entirely rebuilding Hampton Court, and in 1695 instructed Wren to proceed with the construction of a new range across the two south pavilions at Kensington, a project which had already figured in a plan of Wren's of 1690, and which the King must have discussed with his wife. Along the upper

floor ran the King's Gallery, 96 feet long, the noblest room
in the palace, for which William Kent painted the ceiling
panels in 1725–7.

The new building has proved the making of the Palace,
and of the view from the south-east familiar to Londoners.
The original windows, carved door-surrounds, and decorated
cornice of the gallery are still in place, and attest the skill of
Grinling Gibbons, whose work in 'The New Gallery' and
other rooms of the Palace in the period 1691–6 are charged
in the Work's Account at the substantial sum of £839. John
Churchill, the carpenter, put in a large bill of £3,939 which
was principally for work in the new building. By contrast,
Robert Norden's fee for 'drawing a Mapp for the Chimny
peece, and for attending the Painters', seems moderate at £5.
This map of north-west Europe can still be seen in the gallery,
forming part of an interesting wind-dial marked with the
points of the compass, the direction of the prevailing wind
being indicated by a revolving pointer worked by rods con-
nected with a wind-vane on the roof. Like the weather-vane
on the clock-tower, it is a reminder of William's preoccu-
pation with the Continent and of the tactical importance
of wind changes, which, among other things, affected the
arrival of dispatches from Holland. The wind-dial still
functions (1968), and on windy days the pointer oscillates
wildly. According to Macaulay, it was admired by Peter the
Great.

In William's day the gallery, which now houses a collection
of London topographical paintings, was hung with the finest
pictures in the royal collection. The stately room was his
pride. After a riding accident at Hampton Court, on 21 February 1702, William returned to Kensington to nurse a broken
collar-bone. On 3 March he walked in his gallery, and fell
asleep by an open window looking out over the park. When he
awoke he was suffering from a chill; he developed a cough and

a temperature; his lungs were affected. A day or two afterwards he died.

William and Mary have scarcely been appreciated as they
deserve. It will be appropriate in the next chapter to consider
this anxious couple, whose English affections were centred in
each other and in Kensington Palace.

2 · WILLIAM AND MARY

England's constitutional rights and religious establishment stem from William III and Mary II to an extent even greater than is generally recognized. There are two different versions of the legend on the banner flying at the masthead of Prince William's flagship which landed him at Brixham in 1688. In translation, it read either 'For Religion and Liberty – I will maintain', or 'The Liberties of England and the Protestant Religion'. The second version is the more specific, and corresponds to William's faithful achievement.

The Convention that governed England after the flight of James II offered the crown to William and Mary as equal sovereigns during their joint and separate lives, though William was to control the administration so long as he lived. The Declaration of Rights summarized the conditions under which they were to reign; the sovereign could not exact money from his subjects or maintain a standing army in time of peace without the consent of Parliament; the right to free elections and freedom of parliamentary debate was proclaimed, also the right of the subject to petition and to receive impartial justice. Here is the basis of English government as we know it today; and that the Dutch have since proved our most reliable friends on the continent is no coincidence.

Indebted though we have been to their dispensation, William and Mary remained for 250 years remote and unsympathetic figures. Superficially, William appeared as retired, cold and melancholy; Mary as the shadow of her husband, amiable but ineffectual. Recent writers like Dr Nesca Robb, Miss Hester Chapman, and Dr Maurice Ashley, using the new and more patient understanding of complexity which is one of our modern virtues, have torn up these misleading judgments. Far from being dull, William and Mary are now revealed not only as conscientious rulers but as interesting and intensely human young people. He was fifty-two when he died, she only thirty-two.

Both were grandchildren of Charles I. The memory of their grandfather's tragedy hung over them, and recurred to their minds like a periodic nightmare. William, born in 1650, was the posthumous son of William II of Orange by Princess Mary Henrietta; his father had done all he could for his ill-fated father-in-law, and his mother had loyally supported her brother Charles II. His cousin, Mary II, born in 1662, who became William's wife when she was fifteen, was the daughter of his uncle James II by Anne Hyde. In fact, the 'Glorious Revolution' of 1688 resulted from a family quarrel, in which the new King replaced his uncle and father-in-law, and the new Queen supplanted her father. It was also much more than that. William was, first of all, a loyal Dutchman. He stoutly resisted Louis XIV of France in the field; and with his Presbyterian upbringing, he watched with alarm the manœuvres of the Roman Catholic James II. He feared not only that Louis XIV might gain control of England, but that James's untrustworthiness might lead to the fall of the English monarchy and the triumph of republicanism.

William won his bloodless victory because he was a stronger character, more courageous, more determined, more intelligent than his weak, dissipated father-in-law. Disaffection sapped the resolution of James's army and navy; his chief supporters went over to William's side. The English sensed that William's leadership offered them the compromise solution of a limited monarchy, a free parliament, and freedom from papistry. Their instinct has been justified by three centuries of stable democracy. Whether William be viewed as a high-principled idealist or a shrewd statesman – and he was both – his intervention has proved far-reaching indeed; with

William III.
Oil painting from the studio of
W. Wissing.

Queen Mary II.
Oil painting by J. Closterman.

PLATE I

Queen Anne and Knights of
the Garter at Kensington
Palace, 4 August, 1713.
Detail from oil painting by
Peter Angelis (see p. 28).

PLATE II

George I.
Detail from oil painting from
the studio of Sir Godfrey
Kneller (see p. 30).

the hindsight of three hundred years, it is hardly too much to describe this revolution as 'glorious'.

William and Mary had a constant struggle against ill-health. In person, William was small and frail, with a countenance of aristocratic distinction. Weakened by smallpox as a young man, he became a chronic asthma sufferer, often looked shockingly ill, and kept himself going by will power. With his lofty ideals and perpetual anxieties, he was under continual nervous strain, and when he relaxed he could fall into abstraction. There is a famous story that on an occasion when Princess Anne – whose slowness exasperated him – dined with him and Mary, he mechanically ate up all the green peas in the dish. But William's outward taciturnity was not a true reflection of the man. He could be sociable (though not gregarious) and kind, even 'very merry'. Temperamentally inclined to melancholy, he worked so hard and so patiently that it is not surprising that he should have sought recuperation in retirement. He was at his best in the open air, on horseback, on one of his military campaigns, or planning a new estate. In moments of dejection, he depended greatly on friends like H. W. Bentinck (Earl of Portland) and Arnold Keppel (Earl of Albemarle). Burdened with an incessant cough, and probably in later years with pernicious anaemia, there is little doubt that much of his illness would nevertheless be diagnosed nowadays as 'psychosomatic'.

The explanation may partly be found in his domestic life, where he was a victim of the 'eternal triangle'. He loved his wife, who grew into a beauty, but her miscarriages disappointed him of a child, and her general weakness soon made him discontented. He acquired a mistress, but not casually

a

or without remorse; Elizabeth Villiers was never flaunted and remains a shadowy figure, to whom in 1693 he granted some Irish property. Mary was the love of his life; and after her death William lived austerely, consoled by his religion, according to his true nature. Sexually, we may perhaps diagnose an ambivalent character, with some homosexual leanings. There was much to endear him to those who knew him well enough to understand his goodness and complexity.

Mary herself shared her husband's piety and his artistic tastes (he formed a notable picture collection); she was skilled in needlework and painting; they had in common a love of flowers and gardens, and of a quiet existence. She adored her husband, and though she suffered great pain when she discovered the truth about Elizabeth Villiers, she seems, after the first shock, to have reconciled herself to their relationship, which probably did not continue to be a guilty one after the Court came to England. At the hour of William's departure from Holland in 1688, the couple realized their mutual dependence. 'During the whole interview,' said Mary, 'he showed me all the tenderness that I could have desired – so much indeed, that all my life I shall never forget it.' She told William that she had never loved any man but him. When they were reunited in London, she wept to see him so worn; but it was her grace and cheerfulness that made up for William's temperamental deficiencies, and consolidated the public acceptance of the new régime.

During the disturbed six years of her reign, while William was often absent in Ireland and on the Continent, fighting the war against his father-in-law and the French, Mary administered the government with marked success. 'Do but continue to love me,' she wrote to her husband in September 1690, 'and forgive the taking up so much of your time to your poor wife, who deserves more pity than ever any creature did, and who loves you a great deal too much for her ease, though it can't be more than you deserve.'

The progress of the alterations at Kensington formed a link between the separated couple. Mary delighted to encourage her husband to think of the Palace as a future refuge, to take the place of the small Dutch country residences such as Het Loo which he so much enjoyed. She complains of the 'fideling' work on the outside of the house, which meant that the windows had to be kept boarded, and suggests how they could contrive to sleep there while their rooms were still unfinished – the fact of 'our being there' would stimulate the workmen. She writes from Whitehall, in August 1690, that Kensington 'looks really very well, at least to a poor body like me, who have been so long condemned to this place, and see nothing but water or walls'.

Mary busied herself in the gardens at Kensington, to the south of the Palace, now bare slopes of grass* but arranged at that time in formal Dutch patterns, with yew and box. Defoe writes: 'The first laying out of these Gardens was the Design of the late Queen *Mary*, who finding the Air agreed with, and was necessary to the Health of the King, resolved to make it agreeable to her self too, and gave the first Orders for enlarging the Gardens: the Author of this Account, having had the Honour to attend Her Majesty, when she first viewed the Ground, and directed the doing it, speaks this with the more Satisfaction.'

Mary also collected china, and in the Queen's Gallery at Kensington had no fewer than 154 pieces, housed in handsome cabinets, one of which 'of fine marketree' is still in the royal collection. Damask, silk and velvet were used for curtains and upholstery.

* They were cleared in the seventeen-thirties.

William found 'an incorrigible slowness and negligence' among the English – the phrase has a familiar sound – and the English, for their part, did not hasten to show gratitude to their foreign saviour. The happiest glimpses that we have of him are at Kensington. Significantly, both concern children, whose presence William always welcomed, having none of his own. Anne's precocious but short-lived son, the Duke of Gloucester, was a favourite. At the age of four he twice paraded an army of little boys at Kensington for the King's inspection. William played his part splendidly, and Gloucester told him: 'My dear King, you shall have both my companies with you to Flanders.' Young Lord Buckhurst was another friend, who was playing with a toy cart in the corridors of the Palace when he knocked on the King's door. 'Who is that?' 'It's Lord Buck.' 'And what does Lord Buck want with me?' asked William. 'The Queen says you're to come to tea now,' was the reply. The King seized the boy, put him in the cart, and ran with him to the Queen's drawing-room, where he subsided speechless with a fit of coughing.

Such private episodes best show, it may be thought, the King's real character. And the same can be said of two other very different scenes at Kensington.

The story of Mary's death from smallpox at Kensington in December 1694 is undeniably harrowing. For William her last illness proved a shattering experience. 'You can imagine what a state I am in, loving her as I do,' he wrote to the Prince de Vaudemont. 'You know what it is to have a good wife.' He had his camp-bed set up in Mary's crowded bedroom, but found little rest on it. When he did manage for a time to stop coughing, the Queen noticed it, and asked where he was.

She looked round the room, saying, 'Why are you crying? I am not very bad.' As he came to realize that no hope remained, William told Bishop Burnet: 'From being the happiest, I am going to be the miserablest creature upon earth. I have never known a single fault in her!' Towards the end, William collapsed with a nervous breakdown, and for months his health caused great anxiety. He could not stay at Kensington, but temporarily shut himself up in dejection in a house on Richmond Green.

Yet when the King in turn faced death, eight years later, after the fall from his horse at Hampton Court, it was surely not by chance that he found himself again in Kensington Palace, where he had known more happiness than anywhere else in England. In his exhaustion, he had no heart for the final struggle against pneumonia. With resignation, he capitulated, saying, 'Je tire vers ma fin.' After his death, a ring containing a lock of Mary's hair was found fastened to his left arm by a black ribbon. The locket was removed – a sadly insensitive action. This love token symbolized the essential truth of his life, and should have been buried with him.

William properly has his Kensington memorial. His sculptured figure is well sited in front of Wren's south wing and the King's Gallery; but unfortunately William still keeps his distance from the people, for the statue is placed so far inside the railing that they cannot see it properly. Its origin could also provoke a cynical comment; the work of a German, H. Baucke, it was presented to Edward VII by the German Kaiser in 1907. But it is a good statue.

3 · QUEEN ANNE

'King William thinks all,
Queen Mary talks all,
Prince George drinks all,
And Princess Anne eats all.'

The doggerel lines, written shortly after the Revolution of 1688, have a certain elementary biographical truth. They are amplified by the remark of a Tory M.P., Sir John Packington, after the announcement of the death of King William: 'Sir, we have lost a great King; we have got a most gracious Queen.'

William had been an impartial ruler, but the Tories had never forgotten that he owed his throne to the Whigs; they looked forward eagerly to the accession of an Anglican High Churchwoman. Anne herself – William's sister-in-law, and the second daughter of James II – had never liked William, whom she called 'Mr Caliban', and she recognized her own Tory sympathies; nevertheless, she was as committed as her predecessor to the war with the French, holding it her first duty to win it. Believing that William's horse had stumbled over a molehill when he suffered his fatal fall, the Jacobites toasted the 'little gentleman in black velvet'. But the Jacobites received no comfort from the new Queen.

She pleasantly surprised her subjects from the beginning – by addressing her Privy Council on 8 March 1702 in a clear and attractive speaking voice. She continued to surprise them by showing that, for all her slowness and dowdiness and ill-health, she possessed a mind of her own, good sense tempered by humanity, and an appealing Englishness. Her favourite, Sarah, Duchess of Marlborough – the quick and witty Whig – held the attraction of all opposites; but Anne found the strength to put her in her place at last; the overwrought friendship of 'Mrs Morley' and 'Mrs Freeman' came to an abrupt end.

Anne renewed the mystery of the monarchy by reviving the practice of touching for the 'Queen's Evil', a piece of magic that William had sternly rejected; young Samuel Johnson was one of those brought to be touched, and had 'a confused but somehow a sort of solemn recollection of a lady in diamonds and a long black hood.' And Anne exercised her royal prerogative of mercy with conscientious care, ordering many reprieves from the death sentence.

All things considered, she may be forgiven for enjoying a good appetite. Her tendency to obstinacy could have been a more serious failing. This showed itself early in her reign, when for two months she tried to get her stolid blond husband, Prince George of Denmark, chosen as leader of the Allied Army in the Low Countries. The Dutch resisted the proposal, and fortunately the appointment went to the Duke of Marlborough. The Queen's misguided attempt is evidence of her affection for her husband, who soon afterwards was content to become the nominal Lord High Admiral; luckily George had no political ambitions, and was perfectly willing to take a back seat. It was a happy marriage; the couple always shared the same bedroom. George was not clever, but he was kind and faithful; his only fault was that he drank a great deal; Charles II compared him to 'a Great Jarr or Vessel standing still & receiving unmoved & undisturbed so much liquor whenever it came to his turn'.

Queen Anne, the younger daughter of James II and Anne Hyde, born in 1664, was in her late thirties when she came to the throne. In England a rare combination of national talents was approaching fulfilment; the military brilliance of Marl-borough, the scientific genius of Newton, writers from Swift and Defoe to Addison, Pope and Congreve, architects like Wren and Vanbrugh were all to shed their glory on this short reign. But the Queen's faith and constancy, transcending obstinacy, were to set the example – and Kensington Palace, was, more often than not, to provide the scene for her hours of crisis.

Health was denied to Anne and her husband, as it had been to their predecessors William and Mary; despite her frequent pregnancies, she left no heir after the little Duke of Gloucester had died; for her, the trials of a gouty constitution, and possibly of arthritis, had to be encountered daily, while Prince George's asthmatic cough became as familiar at Kensington as King William's had been. During the negotiations in 1706 for one of the chief triumphs of her reign, the Act of Union between England and Scotland, Sir John Clerk, a Scottish Commissioner, twice visited Queen Anne in her small closet at Kensington. Expecting to see a picture-book Queen, he was appalled to discover the suffering woman of reality, 'in extreme pain and agony', with a face 'red and spotty', untidily dressed, her foot swathed in 'nasty bandages'. 'What are you, poor mean like Mortal,' reflected Clerk, 'who talks in the style of a Sovereign?' Yet her homely welcome and her grace-ful speech to the Commissioners impressed him. He recalled that it was not the first time that women had governed in Britain, 'and indeed they have sometimes done this to better purpose than the men'.

At Kensington Anne is remembered for her alterations in the Palace gardens. Having previously lived for some time in the neighbourhood, at Campden House, she was pleased to have the Palace as her residence, but she did not admire what Thomas Faulkner called the 'tiresome uniformity' of William's Dutch gardens, and determined to make them more English, setting her great gardener Henry Wise to work rooting up the box and shrubs. In about 1705 Wise prepared a plan (Plate VI) for the development of a series of separate pools along the course of the West Bourne river, which eventually became the Serpentine, and he envisaged a small oblong pool, which later took shape as the Round Pond; but these developments were not realized until long after Anne's death. Wise, however, raised and levelled the land to the east of the house, the future site of the Round Pond, fitted it with borders, turf and gravel, and stocked it with flowers and evergreens. He took in a paddock there that was previously parkland. But his most immediately effective area of work lay to the north of the Palace, the eastern part being treated as a formal wilderness, and the western split into subdivisions with radial paths stretching to the Bayswater Road. Not a trace remains of this 'Upper Garden', which must have been delightful in its time. Wise's inventions included an artificial mount and a sunk garden* made out of a gravel-pit. 'It must have been a fine Genius for Gardening,' wrote Addison in *The Spectator* in 1712, 'that could have thought of forming such an unsightly Hollow into so beautiful an Area and to have hit the Eye with so uncommon and agreeable a Scene. . . .'

While Wise was engaged in making the 'Upper Garden', the graceful Orangery, which fortunately survives, was being built to the north of the Palace in 1704–6, to the joint design apparently of Sir Christopher Wren and Sir John Vanbrugh. A letter from Vanbrugh to Lord Godolphin shows that Wren had difficulty in placating his colleague, who was exasperated by the devious practices of the Office of Works. It has been suggested that the Orangery was originally intended to form part of an annexed wing to the Palace itself, to be used for State receptions, but this hardly seems likely. The Orangery

*To be distinguished from the present sunken garden immediately to the east of the Palace, which was constructed in 1909.

was the scene of a number of dinner-parties given by Anne and her husband, when music would be played in one of the rooms at each end. No building in the country epitomizes the spirit of Anne's England so completely as the Kensington Orangery – indeed in its elegance it is much more characteristic than the Queen's only other notable architectural commission, Blenheim Palace at Woodstock. It may never have grown oranges, but in 1820 it contained lemons, gum trees and other exotic plants.

One item in the Kensington Palace accounts for 1702–8 seems to refer to the massive Alcove designed by Wren which formerly stood near the Kensington Road, closing the vista down the path opposite the south wing: 'Paid to John Smoute, *Mason*, Work done & Stone used at the *New Summerhouse at the lower end of the Garden*, £555 7s. 9d.' The Alcove, with Queen Anne's initials over the arch, now stands near the Fountain Garden at the head of the Serpentine. One has the feeling that it has lost its way, but at best it was an extravagant device for sheltering a small number of people, (see endpapers).

Anne's restricted domestic life was dominated by the women around her, whose attitudes were conditioned in turn by a complex political situation. She had been captivated by Sarah Jennings, later Duchess of Marlborough, since she was a child of six (Sarah being four years older). The timid lymphatic Anne found inspiration and encouragement in Sarah's toughness and vitality. Sarah married young; and when Anne appointed her First Lady of the Bedchamber, she decided that they should correspond informally under assumed names; Anne became 'Mrs Morley', Sarah, 'Mrs Freeman', and Marlborough of course was 'Mr Freeman'. The very whimsicality of the notion carried its dangers and presaged ultimate disillusion, but for many years hundreds of fussy, affectionate, self-pitying, and, alas, tedious letters went from Anne to Sarah, sometimes as often as twice a day. 'Upon my word,' wrote Anne at an early stage, 'I cannot live without you. . . .' And this became increasingly true, however much she might 'wish you and Mr Freeman every thing your own harts can desire'. Both women suffered from gout or arthritis, and Anne was continually urging Sarah to drink ass's milk; Marlborough also had to try it, but it 'soe disorder'd mee' that he took 'a resolution of leaving itt off'.

At the beginning of the reign, Sarah, soon appointed Groom of the Stole, was extremely helpful in giving Anne the confidence to rule. Both Marlborough and Lord Godolphin ('Mr Montgomery'), her first Prime Minister, were moderate Tories, who shrewdly managed a coalition with the Whigs that lasted for eight years. As time went on, political pressures upset this tight confederacy. In 1704 Anne was overjoyed to learn of the victory of Blenheim, which assured England of her independence and of a century of civilized progress and taste: 'I have had the happiness,' she wrote to Sarah, 'of receiving my dear Mrs Freeman's, by Colonel Parke, with the good news of this glorious victory which, next to God Almighty, is wholly owing to dear Mr Freeman, on whose safety I congratulate you with all my soul.' The great palace of Blenheim was commissioned from Vanbrugh as 'Mr Freeman's' reward and its model was shown to the Queen in the King's Gallery at Kensington. Marlborough's soldiers marched to further victories:

'Over the hills and over the main
To Flanders, Portugal and Spain,
Queen Anne commands and we'll obey,
Over the hills and far away.'

But in those days the Whigs were the war party; they received the support of the influential Sarah; inevitably their power increased with England's military triumphs. Godolphin turned Whig, taking into his government the Whig Earl of Sunderland, Marlborough's son-in-law. The war went on, but Anne's anxiety grew as her country began to long for peace.

Robert Harley, Earl of Oxford, the Tory leader, found a friend on the backstairs at court to offset the domination of Sarah. She was Abigail Hill, a junior lady-in-waiting (who became Mrs Masham, and afterwards Lady Masham). On her Christmas visit to Kensington in 1707, Sarah noted that Anne 'stood all the while' and looked 'coldly upon me'. Victories now gave the Queen no pleasure, and when she was told the news of Oudenarde, she said 'Oh, Lord, when will all this dreadful bloodshed cease?'

When it was known, in October 1708, that Prince George was dying, Sarah went to Kensington. After his death, she persuaded the Queen, despite her evident reluctance, to move temporarily to St James's. But the friendship of years had now been shattered, and Sarah found it 'very shocking' that Anne should have commanded: 'Send to Masham to come to me before I go.' Overwhelmed with grief, the Queen clearly found more understanding in Mrs Masham than in the Duchess. In her chagrin, Sarah noted that, as they left the Palace, 'she had strength to bend down towards Mrs Masham like a sail and in passing by went some steps more than was necessary to be nearer her'. It was an obvious sign – as reliable as William's wind-dial – of a change of favour.

Sarah, in her hardness, scarcely believed that the Queen could show such grief at the death of her dull husband. Anne told her that she had requested the Lord Treasurer that, 'when he sends his orders to Kensington, he would give directions there may be a great many yeomen of the guards to carry the prince's dear body, that it may not be let fall, the great stairs being very steep and slippery'. Anne may have remembered the accident on the stairs after Queen Mary's death, but the Queen's note only made Sarah smile.

Mrs Masham was allowed to move into Sarah's rooms at Kensington. The Duchess wrote long reproachful letters. Sarah still kept her offices, for her husband was needed to win the battle of Malplaquet; but the Queen was soon telling him that 'I believe nobody was ever so used by a friend . . . I desire nothing but that she would leave off teasing & tormenting me. . . .' Their last interview approached inevitably. It took place on 6 April 1710, in one of the Queen's little closets at Kensington, where she now spent much of her time because they held the most intimate memories of her husband. The haughty Sarah asked to be told of what she was accused. Fastening on words that Sarah had used in a letter, the Queen repeated over and over again: 'You desired no Answer, and you shall have none.' Sarah wept, and said that Anne would suffer for her inhumanity. 'The Queen answer'd, that will be to myself.'

Dismissals of Lord Godolphin and the Earl of Sunderland followed swiftly on the humiliation of the Duchess; that of Marlborough himself came in due course. The Tories returned to power; Swift's pamphleteering convinced the country that the Marlboroughs had prolonged the war for their own advantage. But, for all Sarah's shortcomings, we must face the paradox that the years of Anne's greatness were those of her alliance with 'Mrs Freeman'. As a final thrust, Sarah claimed £16,000 from the Queen for back pay. The claim was allowed. Sarah admitted that she 'did not much like doing this', but solaced herself with the reflection that she had earned the money by many hours of boredom.

. . . . . .

The remainder of Queen Anne's reign was largely devoted to securing a general peace, rendered more than ever necessary by the failure of the Spanish campaign. It was a slow process, both at home and abroad, and at one stage, in 1712, she had to create twelve new Tory peers to overcome opposition in the House of Lords. One of these was Mrs Masham's husband. Marlborough was retired in disgrace, after charges of corruption had been laid against him which, if partly justified, left the Queen and her government with the stigma of ingratitude. All this was a high price to pay for the Treaty of Utrecht, signed in the summer of 1713, and for Tory success at the general election which followed. In August, 1713, an installation of Knights of the Garter was held at Kensington, as the Queen was not well enough to go to Windsor (Plate II).

The problem of the Succession now occupied the thoughts of Tories and Whigs alike. In July 1714 Queen Anne became mortally ill; Parliament being in recess, the future of the Crown lay with the Privy Council. Anne's last official act on 30 July, as she lay dying at Kensington, was to appoint as her Treasurer the Duke of Shrewsbury, who could be relied on to procure the lawful Protestant succession of the House of Hanover under the Act of Settlement of 1701. 'The Queen about one o'clock,' we read in the Wentworth Papers, 'gave the Treasurer's staff to the Duke of Shrewsbury, my Lord Chancellor holding her hand to direct it to the Duke.' It is doubtful whether she was fully conscious, but the gesture is what she would have wished, for her love of the Church of England had overcome any lingering Jacobite sympathies.

While the Privy Council's messengers rode through the gate of Kensington Palace, bearing letters designed to secure the country against a Jacobite rising, while troops were called out, and the arms of Roman Catholics seized, the Queen entered on her final sleep. She died on 1 August, a lonely unhappy woman, the last of our Stuart sovereigns. The simple slow-moving Anne had done her duty to the end. She left her country prosperous, Protestant and free.

4 · GEORGE I

A popular Tory historian like Charles Oman, from whom a whole generation before 1914 learned its history, felt no qualms about slapping crisp critical adjectives on to King William III and Queen Anne. These have since been either qualified or removed by better historians such as G. M. Trevelyan. But when we come to reconsider Anne's successor, George I (Plate II), in the hope of dissipating a few unworthy prejudices, we find it impossible to do anything for him, or to disagree with Oman's verdict that he 'was a selfish, hard-hearted, unamiable, and uninteresting man of fifty-four'. The brief for the defence has to be returned; the pink ribbon tied up with a sigh.

The Act of Settlement of 1701 was a political measure, passed in the virtual certainty that neither William nor Anne would produce an heir to the throne, and with the determination of Whigs and Tories alike (at that time) that Jacobitism must be eliminated and the favourable balance of power in Europe maintained. The obligations of the Act were accepted by the Dowager Electress Sophia of Hanover – a grand-daughter of James I of England and a woman of intellect and character – on behalf of herself and her children, of whom her son George was the reigning Elector. Important clauses assured the continuance of the Protestant established Church and laid down that no foreigner could become a Privy Councillor, or an M.P., or enjoy any office or grant of 'lands, tenements, or hereditaments' from the Crown. The repeal of two further clauses in 1705 had the effect of allowing the Parliamentary Cabinet system to develop under the House of Hanover.

The best that can be said of George I is that he interfered little in English politics, and became a constitutional monarch

George II.
Oil painting after Sir Godfrey Kneller (see p. 44).

PLATE III

Queen Caroline of Ansbach, wife of
George II.
Oil painting from the studio of C. Jervas
(see p. 44).

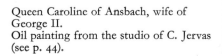

John, Lord Hervey, 1696–1743.
Oil painting by Thomas Hudson
(see pp. 47, 57 and 64).

Horace Walpole, 1717–97.
Oil painting by Sir Joshua Reynolds
(see pp. 57 and 64).

PLATE IV

in the modern sense. This was a matter of necessity rather than of choice; he was completely ignorant of the politics of his new kingdom, and could not speak a word of English. All he knew was that he depended on the Whigs to thwart the Jacobites; he put himself entirely in their hands, discussing affairs of State with his Prime Minister, Sir Robert Walpole, in bad Latin. It all went surprisingly well – as it has done, in less extreme conditions, ever since.

Apart from political shrewdness, of a negative kind, and some personal courage, George was a dull unpleasant man. He was selfish, sensual and immoral; he drank heavily of punch, and, like many Germans, he was far too fond of his food. He was unfaithful to his wife Sophia, and treated her most cruelly after their divorce by confining her in the castle of Ahlden. He neglected his mother and detested his son, who became George II. When Saussure, a French gentleman, visited him in 1725, he found him 'short of stature and very corpulent, his cheeks are pendent and his eyes are too big, he looks kind and amiable, but those who do not like him say that he is not generous in money matters. . . .'

George brought over from Hanover a household of about a hundred people, who effectively insulated him from his English subjects. They included the statesmen Bernsdorff and Bothmer, and his secretary Robethon, who had a great deal of power; there were also his two Turkish servants, various doctors, cooks, trumpeters and cellarmen, and a chaplain, a plate-cleaner and a washerwoman. Most important of all was his mistress, Ermengarda Melusina von Schulenberg, Duchess of Kendal. According to Lord Chesterfield, George liked his women to be fat; but, if this is true, the Duchess of Kendal was an exception to the rule, for she was thin, and not particularly beautiful. Another German woman who exercised considerable influence at court was the Baroness von Kilmansegge, whom he created Countess of Darlington.

It was thought at the time that she, too, was the King's mistress, but this is not certain; she may, indeed, have been his illegitimate half-sister.

The King's German followers were out to enrich themselves as much as possible, and sought by every means to circumvent the Act of Settlement, which had been designed to prevent this happening. George gave the Duchess of Kendal the emoluments of the vacant post of Master of the Horse, and she herself conducted a flourishing trade in State appointments. The London crowd soon came to resent the behaviour of the Duchess. There is a story that they hooted her in the street, and that she put her head out of the coach window and protested: 'Vy do you abuse us, we only come for your goots!' To which a voice from the crowd is supposed to have responded, 'Aye, damn ye, and for our chattels also.' True or false, the dialogue expressed the reality of the situation.

George's reign was notable for the evolution of Cabinet governments, and for an increasing national prosperity which served to disguise his personal shortcomings. It was not an uplifting period, but in the history of Kensington Palace it was significant. The King liked Kensington; the country house and its gardens reminded him of his own home of Herrenhausen in Hanover. He therefore spent as much time there as possible, though the permanent staff at Kensington was small, consisting of the housekeeper, the housekeeper's personal servant, a necessary woman, a sweeper, two watchmen, a bell-ringer, a man to pump water, a locksmith and a joiner. The King's own servants accompanied him wherever he went. But for one who expected pomp and circumstance,

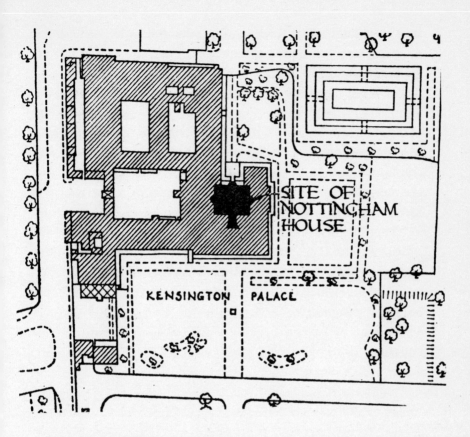

Plan showing relation of Nottingham House to the present Palace
buildings.

Kensington Palace was not quite grand enough. Eventually he set about its enlargement.

Old Nottingham House finally disappeared, after a survey by Nicholas Hawksmoor in 1718, which resulted in the order 'that the Old Body of the House, that is very ruinous and out of Repair and wants rebuilding, be carefully considered of'. The Minutes of the Office of Works in 1718–19 contain several references to 'the New Brickworke His Majesty has been pleased to order'; incidentally, 'the seats made for the Musicians in the Greenhouse' (the Orangery) were ordered to be removed. Sir Christopher Wren was dismissed from his post of surveyor, and his inefficient successor William Benson became responsible for the three new State Rooms on the upper floor of the building that superseded Nottingham House; these may have been inspired by an earlier plan of Vanbrugh's. The new rooms were originally known as the Drawing Room, Privy Chamber, and Cube Room (or Cupola Room), and are so identified in a book of plans of Royal Apartments in the Royal Library at Windsor.

The central Cupola Room is the most important of the new rooms, being intended as the main reception-room. It was decorated in 1722, in a style of ornate grandeur, by William Kent. The walls are ornamented by Ionic pilasters; there is a heavy marble chimney-piece, and pedestals and niches hold gilded statues; in the ceiling is an octagonal panel painted with the star of the Order of the Garter: the whole representing a resounding example of the heavy taste of the period. The other new rooms, also decorated by Kent, are slightly less overpowering, and Kent's ceilings have more merit than they have usually been allowed.

The new State Rooms were so badly built by William Benson that in 1724 £1,925 had to be spent in repairing them, as they were 'in great danger'. In 1725 or earlier further major rebuilding was carried out on the north side of Clock

Court, affecting the kitchens and also involving the irregular 'office' buildings to the west of the Queen's Gallery. Two improved courtyards were devised with arcaded cloisters: the Prince of Wales's Court to the west and the Princesses' Court (Plate XVI) to the east, bounded on the north by the rooms of the Maids of Honour. In the north range of the western court a handsome apartment was erected on three floors: this was intended for the Duchess of Kendal. The French Ambassador, Count Broglie, states that the King was in the habit of visiting her there between five and eight o'clock in the evening, when she would act as a go-between for those desirous of the King's patronage. In an article in *Country Life* (1 September 1928), Mr Christopher Hussey has suggested that Thomas Ripley, master carpenter to the Board of Works, may have been the architect of the courtyards. We know that he applied for, and received, 'riding charges' to Kensington.

Another suggestion contained in the *Country Life* article of 1928 is that the Princesses' Court was named after the young daughters of George I's son, the Prince of Wales. The King had a violent quarrel with his son that resulted in an almost total breakdown of contact between them from 1717 to 1720. The Prince was expelled from the royal palaces, and he and his wife were forbidden the custody of their own children, for whom the King appointed a governess, the Duchess of Portland. At first, the children stayed at St James's Palace; but it was conceded that the youngest, a delicate boy born in 1717, required his mother's care, and she was allowed to take him to Kensington, where he died in 1718.

In that year the Judges decided by a majority that the King had absolute control over his grandchildren. In 1718 the three daughters, Anne, Emily and Caroline, were nine, eight, and five years old; and it appears that they were lodged for a time in the house of the Maids of Honour which looks out on to the eastern court, originally called Pump Court. One would not have imagined that they remained there after the Prince of Wales and his wife were established at Leicester House and Richmond Lodge, following his reconciliation with his father in 1720. However, an Office of Works minute book of 1723-4 contains two entries: 'The young Princesses' Gallery to be panelled', and 'For making a way from the Duchess of Kendall's to the young Princesses' Lodging'. The Lord Chamberlain also instructs the Office of Works 'to build two rooms over the new arcade in Green Cloth Court for the Duchess of Kendall and two closets for the young princesses, and one for the Countess of Portland.' These entries serve to confirm the connection of the princesses with Kensington Palace, although the length and circumstances of their residence remain obscure. The closets mentioned may have been in an additional block attached to the westward side of the Queen's Gallery; it is distinguishable by the different coloured brickwork, and one room can be approached from what is identified within the Palace as Apartment No. 10, of which it now forms part.

The attractive arcaded courtyards have remained virtually unaltered externally, apart from war damage, since they attained their final form in the seventeen-twenties. The whole of the western wing of Prince of Wales's Court, probably named after the temporary residence of the Prince of Wales ('poor Fred'), was then given up to kitchens and bake-houses, later incorporated in Apartment 4, and a row of single-storey outhouses was constructed, which are still standing behind the boundary wall on the Palace Green side. The interior of Apartment 8 (the Duchess of Kendal's residence) was decorated by William Kent, the plasterwork on the stair-case and the chimney-pieces being particularly notable. Restored in 1899-1900, this house unfortunately now stands empty in a sad state of dilapidation, as it has never been repaired since the roof was damaged in 1940. Apartment 9, which divides the two courtyards, was also severely damaged in the Second World War, and awaits restoration. Work of this kind has been more than ever hampered in recent years by cuts in Government expenditure.

The most interesting of Kent's decorative paintings were those for the Grand Staircase (Plate V), to which he gave its final form in the seventeen-twenties, altering Wren's windows, covering the walls and ceiling with paintings, and extending the upper landing. On the north wall he painted an arcaded gallery with a marble balustrade, behind which groups of people closely associated with the court look out over the stairs. Among these can be identified some Yeomen of the Guard and George's two Turkish servants, while a group on the east wall includes Peter the Wild Boy. The latter was found in the woods near Hamelin in Hanover in 1725. He was then about thirteen, and, according to Faulkner, he walked on his hands and feet, climbed trees 'with the agility of a squirrel', and fed on grass and moss. Peter was presented to King George, who brought him to England and exhibited him as a curiosity. His contribution to court life seems to have been small; he was 'with difficulty persuaded to lie on a bed', and he 'resisted all instruction'. He was given a pension and lived until 1785.

Altogether, the staircase provides lively and curious period entertainment. This is continued on the ceiling, where Kent painted a number of additional figures peering down, including himself, two of his pupils and 'a beautiful actress', with whom (Faulkner assures us) 'he lived on terms of intimacy'. Kent had difficulty in getting paid for his work on the ceiling of the

'Great Chamber' (presumably the Cupola Room) and 'was made uneasy for want of his money'; thereafter he was paid more regularly, receiving £500 for the 'Drawing Room' and £300 for the ceiling of the 'Privy Chamber'.

The reign of George I – after the summary suppression of the Jacobite rebellion in 1715 – was as uninteresting as the monarch. In no sense a popular sovereign, he was tolerated so long as things went well. A financial crisis like the 'South Sea Bubble' of 1720 brought out the latent animosity against the German court, which was expressed in the following doggerel:

> 'God in his wrath sent Saul to trouble Jewry,
> And George to England in a greater fury;
> For George in sin as far exceedeth Saul
> As ever Bishop Burnet did St Paul.'

For the most part, however, and increasingly latterly, Sir Robert Walpole's aptitude for political and commercial management kept the country quiet. The King saw to the comfort of his mistresses and to the security of his German dominions; he failed entirely to stimulate his British subjects, except possibly by suggesting some satirical material for *Gulliver's Travels*. It seems fitting that he should have died in 1727 at Osnabrück, while on his way to visit Herrenhausen.

But he had laid his hand on Kensington Palace. George I is not an inviting subject for meditation, yet the pompous Cupola Room is an appropriate place to think about him. Nevertheless, he also had his share in the making of Kensington Gardens – those spacious avenues of trees and grass, more French in plan than German, that remain a constant refreshment to Londoners and can still evoke delighted surprise from foreigners. Difficult though it is to like King George, Cabinet government and Kensington Gardens have been substantial benefits.

5 · THE MAKING OF
KENSINGTON GARDENS

It was long held as an indictment against Queen Anne and
George II's consort Queen Caroline that they took 330 acres
from Hyde Park in order to make Kensington Gardens.
This was anyway impossible, because the total acreage of the
Gardens is only 245; but it is founded on a misapprehension –
the parkland of Nottingham House always approximated to
the area of Kensington Gardens, and it was this parkland that
was developed, in small part by Henry Wise and more completely and systematically later.

Wise's tentative plan of about 1705 (Plate VI) indicates the
course of the Broad Walk, and shows the future Round Pond
as a small oblong pool and the Serpentine as a chain of ten
separate basins. Towards the end of George I's reign, but
before 1726, Wise submitted a radical scheme for the park in
partnership with Charles Bridgman; the latter succeeded him
as the royal gardener on Wise's retirement at Lady Day 1728,
and was left to carry out their intentions. The Treasury
accepted an estimate of £3,800 for the making of avenues and
planting of trees; this specified the 'Grand Walk' as being 80
feet wide by 2,800 feet long, about the dimensions of the
Broad Walk. The shape of the 'Great Bow' was then already
settled; and it was all to be 'by His Majesty's own direction'.
Before the death of George I, work had been done to
the value of £1,668. It is certain, then, that although
Queen Caroline interested herself eagerly in the Gardens,
she was not (as has often been stated) responsible for their
inception.

The Round Pond was not finished until the new reign, and
was filled with water in 1728. Kensington Public Library has

an interesting plan which appears to show the state of progress in the Gardens in 1729. They are roughly the same as they are today, except that the Serpentine and its surrounding area is unfinished.

Queen Caroline had a passion for landscape gardening and encouraged all these works, but probably her original responsibility was confined to the Serpentine. Here she appears to have had more extensive designs; the roads to Kensington Palace were muddy, and after the completion of the Round Pond we find suggestions that the Palace was damp; at all events, William Kent made a wooden model for a Palladian Palace in Hyde Park, which is now to be seen at the Victoria and Albert Museum. The *London Journal* of 26 September 1730 contains the announcement: 'Next Monday they begin upon the Serpentine River and Royal Mansion in Hyde Park.' But second thoughts prevailed, and the projected new palace, which would have outraged a public already growing sensitive to London's open spaces, was abandoned on the grounds of expense.

The work of joining together the marshy ponds of the West Bourne was carried out in 1730–1 by Charles Wither, Surveyor-General of His Majesty's Woods, whose bill for making the Serpentine came to £4,755. It was a tremendous job, which involved digging out 74,644 cubic yards of earth from the verge of 'the old waste watercourse', and 'grubbing up in several places, and drawing up upon the hill out of the way of the water-line, 105 large Oaks, Elms, and Willows, at 4d each'. From the paddock surrounding the Round Pond 321 loads of earth were taken to make up the new head or dam. Eighteen horses and sixty men were needed to transplant twenty large elms. The *London Journal* of 1 May 1731 records the completion of the undertaking by declaring: 'Two yachts are to be placed in the Serpentine River in Hyde Park for the diversion of the Royal Family.'

Still more expenses were to come, however, for in 1736–7 the Knightsbridge end of the Serpentine had to be 'secured', the outlet improved, and a receiving lake constructed – all of which cost a further £2,606. It was not until nearly a century later that Rennie's bridge was built over the Serpentine, and the dirty little West Bourne diverted into a sewer, since when the water in the Serpentine has been largely supplied by a well at the Bayswater end. In 1869–70 a vast amount of 'black putrid mud' was removed from the Serpentine, also a lot of fish, which were given temporary asylum in the Round Pond.

A charming small building, probably designed by Kent, which seems to have been erected as part of Bridgman's scheme of 1726–7, is the Queen's Temple in the south-east corner of the Gardens, now incorporated in Temple Lodge. South of the Temple, a mount was made out of the earth excavated for the Serpentine, and this was adorned in 1733 by a revolving summer-house; both are no more.

A plan drawn by John Rocque in 1754 shows Kensington Gardens completed, much as they are today (Plate VI). The Gardens were opened to the public on Saturdays only. This was the day when George II and his court went to Richmond. No one would then go into the Gardens except in 'full dress'. By the time that Thomas Faulkner published his *History and Antiquities of Kensington* (1820), he was able to write: 'They are now open every day, winter and summer, under certain regulations, and the number of the gate-keepers have lately been increased, who are uniformly clothed in green; the great south walk leading to the palace, is crowded on Sunday mornings in the spring and summer, with a display of all the beauty and fashion of the great metropolis, and affords a most gratifying spectacle, not to be equalled in Europe.'

By the time of William IV, the Gardens were open at any

time of year 'to all respectably dressed persons from sunrise to sunset,' a dispensation confirmed by the young Queen Victoria. How they acquired their own literature and statuary, and received their own mythology from James Barrie, can be left to a later stage of this narrative.

6 · GEORGE II AND QUEEN CAROLINE

Court life reached a nadir of dullness under George I. The new reign showed some improvement; it was, at least, more entertaining.

To begin with, George II (Plate III), though not remarkable, was a better man than his father; he was small of stature and inclined to pettiness, his morals were as lax, but he had a sense of justice, loyalty and honesty which engages our sympathy – and a talkative exuberance, verging on absurdity, that keeps him alive. Born in 1684, he received no affection from his father who extended to him the active dislike he had formed for his mother. George Augustus, educated by his grandparents, was considerably spoiled. But, unlike his father, he welcomed his English prospects and looked forward to living in England. His gallantry at Oudenarde, which earned Marlborough's praise, served only to make his father jealous; he was refused any further part in the war.

George differed from his father again in the quality of his marriage. His wedding to Caroline of Anspach (Plate III) in 1705 gave him a good-looking, capable and cultivated wife. Their courtship was a genuine romance, and their mutual affection survived George's naïve infidelities, which were treated by Caroline with realism and tolerance. They were happy in their growing family. The marriage eventually brought to Kensington Palace one of its most attractive queens.

Many people wished to see George Augustus residing in England during the lifetime of Queen Anne, but the proposal encountered too much opposition to be practicable. After his father's accession, however, George and his wife, now the

Prince and Princess of Wales, soon established themselves as favourites in London society. Caroline's grace and charm captivated all who saw her; she made no secret of her liking for her new country, while the Prince praised the English as 'the best, the handsomest, the best shaped, the best natured and the lovingest people in the world'. It is no wonder that the couple were popular, and that England looked hopefully to them to offset its disappointment at the uninspiring George I.

All this aggravated the father's jealousy of his son and led to an open quarrel which lasted for several years. As we have seen, George I even obtained control of his grandchildren. At Leicester House and Richmond Lodge the Princess's entertainments became famous; her guests included Addison, Pope and Gay, and the society she encouraged was much more lively than could be found at court. To contribute to a reconciliation with his father, the Prince tactfully curtailed the scope of his receptions.

After his father's death, George made a perky little King, with agreeable ruddy features, usually genial (though he had a quick temper). He was sensitive to restrictions on his independence and to comments on his wife's superior intelligence, but soon took her advice and submitted to the management of Sir Robert Walpole and the Whig majority. Before long some searching Tory rhymes were being bandied about:

> 'You may strut, dapper George, but 'twill be all in vain;
> We know 'tis Queen Caroline, not you that reign —
> You govern no more than Don Philip of Spain.
> Then if you would have us fall down and adore you,
> Lock up your fat spouse as your Dad did before you!'

This was manifestly unfair, but annoyed him particularly, perhaps because it held an element of truth.

When George II summoned his son Frederick from Hanover in 1728, and made him in turn Prince of Wales, history repeated itself; the boy's easy ways brought him popularity, especially with the Tories, and bred distrust in his father, who was stingy with his allowance. It is a pattern that has since been observed with other Hanoverian sovereigns and their eldest sons, who, bored and flattered, have made themselves objectionable to their parents.

When the King visited Hanover in 1729, Queen Caroline was appointed his sole Regent. At her first Council meeting at Kensington Palace, her commission was read, and the Prince of Wales and all others present 'had the honour to kiss Her Majesty's hand'. If Frederick was a little annoyed at having to knuckle under to his mother, he got over it – for the time being.

Neither the King nor the Queen liked St James's. They spent several months each year at Richmond Lodge, Hampton Court and Windsor. But Kensington was their favourite residence; the place where they felt most at home. The Queen occupied Queen Mary's Gallery and the adjoining rooms, where she had the old Wren panelling painted in white and gold, while the King occupied William's southern suite. A large mahogany cabinet, originally designed as a case for a mechanical organ and harpsichord in about 1735, still stands in the Queen's Gallery.

For members of the staff at Kensington, treatment was more sympathetic in the new reign. A cutting from an unidentified newspaper of 1727, in Kensington Public Library, tells a macabre tale:

'Last Week a Centinel who was just come off of Duty at Kensington, going to the Guard-Room, dropt down as dead. Upon which Notice being sent to his Colonel, he ordered them to take Care and bury him; which was indiscreetly done within a few Hours. But

The Great Staircase at Kensington Palace.
Watercolour by C. Wild, 1819 (see p. 37).

PLATE V

Plan of Kensington Palace Gardens.
By Henry Wise, *c.* 1705 (*Crown Copyright*) (see pp. 23 and 40).

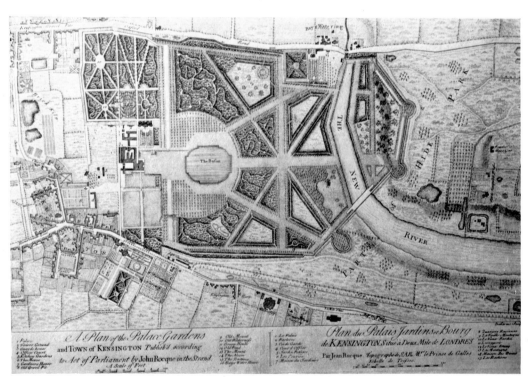

Plan of Kensington Palace Gardens.
By John Rocque, 1754 (*Crown Copyright*) (see p. 42).

PLATE VI

their Majesties hearing of the Affair, as they were at Supper, out of their singular Compassion and great Humanity, immediately ordered him to be taken up again and put into a warm Bed. He bled a little, upon having a Vein open'd, but he had lain too long to be recovered.'

That George II is alive to us in all his littleness and humanity, and Caroline in her good-natured wisdom and realistic accep-tance, is largely due to the Memoirs of John, Lord Hervey (Plate IV). William Pulteney's 'pretty little Master-Miss', and Pope's Lord Fanny – the 'amphibious thing' that 'now trips a lady and now struts a lord' – was of a type still recog-nizable. Uncharitably, he might be described as epicene and corrupt; viewed with more sympathy, he was a chronic invalid, an epileptic, an entertaining gossip, mimic and versifier who became the devoted friend and literary mentor of the Queen, and was tolerated as a useful necessity by the King. Though he has been called chief eunuch of the Palace, and though there are homosexual undertones in his youthful friendship with Stephen Fox, he was married to a beauty and the father of eight children; he was man enough to fight a duel with his traducer Pulteney.

Such, then, was Hervey – viewed with suspicion by many men, popular with most women. His intimate pictures of court life were undeniably authentic; their coarseness reflected the decadence of a reign that gave us Cleland's *Fanny Hill,* a novel gleefully rediscovered in our own age.

Hervey was the repository of court confidences. The King's daughters talked freely to him behind their father's back. Here Anne, the Princess Royal, lets off steam (Hervey always wrote in the third person):

E   47

'One day that the King was extremely out of humour and more than ordinarily froward, Lord Hervey, staying tête-à-tête with the Princess Royal in her apartment at Kensington (the King and Queen and her sisters were walking) said he could not imagine what had made the King so abominably cross all that day, for that no letters were come from abroad, and he did not know of anything that had gone ill at home. "My God!" replied the Princess Royal, "I am ashamed for you, who have been so long about Papa, to know so little of him as when he is the most peevish and snappish to think it is the most material things that have made him so. When great points go as he would not have them, he frets and is bad to himself; but when he is in his worst humours, and the devil to everybody that comes near him, it is always because one of his pages has powdered his periwig ill, or a housemaid set a chair where it does not use to stand, or something of that kind." '

Their Majesties relied on Hervey to supply them with information and political tittle-tattle. Once the Queen 'sent for Lord Hervey whilst she was in bed; and because it was contrary to the queenly etiquette to admit a man to her bedside whilst she was in it, she kept him talking on one side of the door which opened just upon her bed whilst she conversed with him on the other for two hours together, and then sent him to the King's side to repeat to His Majesty all he had related to her'.

At one time Hervey was on such friendly terms with the Prince of Wales that Stephen Fox grew jealous. After Hervey had had a fit in the Queen's drawing-room, the Prince sat with him all day. They wrote ballads and sonnets together, even collaborated in a play. Their friendship declined when Frederick came under the influence of Anne Vane, who had previously been Hervey's mistress. Before long it was clear to Hervey that he must choose between the parents and the son; the choice was not difficult for an ambitious courtier; among other things, it meant admiring the music of Handel, which was favoured by the King and Queen and disliked by the Prince and his friends; the Prince was furious when the Queen gave Hervey a gold snuff-box as a token of her favour.

The break between the Prince and his parents came after his marriage, when he madly asserted his independence by driving his wife, in the last stages of labour, at full gallop from Hampton Court to St James's, so that their child should be born away from their Majesties' surveillance.

It was an insufferable insult; the Prince was expelled from court, and the Queen never saw him again.

Queen Caroline was a good woman, and if she had been able appreciably to influence her husband, he would have been more popular. She showed remarkable generosity; her benefactions to Queen's College, Oxford, are well known, but much of the lavish giving was secret; money flowed out to any cause that appealed to her – £5,000 to the projected Foundling Hospital, £1,000 to the Huguenots who had escaped from French prisons, fifty guineas to a Woolwich drummer's wife who produced triplets, and 'a purse of a gold' to a centenarian in Bushey Park.

The Queen, as Voltaire said, was 'born to encourage'. Her taste and love of art would have had more effect had they been fully shared by her husband; yet they did have a lasting influence. She encouraged the great English architects, and artists such as Kneller and Rysbrack; she tried to patronize Hogarth, but encountered jealousies and wrong-headed criticism; if she had had her way, she would have done still more for the arts. Like Queen Mary in our own century, she made special journeys to visit great houses and collections and artists' studios; the King could not understand it; he thought

49

it undignified and expensive – 'You do not see me running into every puppy's house to see his new chairs and stools,' he said. Her love of gardening found ample scope at Richmond and at Kensington, where she inspired Kent and Bridgman, as we have seen, to implement and extend the existing plans for Kensington Gardens. Here also the money flowed out – £5,000 to Bridgman between 1728 and 1731 for his work at Kensington, with more to come for the Serpentine – too extravagant for the King's liking.

The King's attitude reflected a cooling in his relations with the Queen as she grew older, stouter, and increasingly unwell. One particular disagreement was characteristically recorded by Hervey in 1735:

'In the absence of the King, the Queen had taken several very bad pictures out of the great drawing-room at Kensington, and put very good ones in their places. The King, affecting, for the sake of contradiction, to dislike this change, or, from his extreme ignorance in painting, really disapproving it, told Lord Hervey, as Vice-Chamberlain, that he would have every new picture taken away, and every old one replaced. Lord Hervey, who had a mind to make his court to the Queen by opposing this order, asked if His Majesty would not give leave for the two Vandykes, at least, on each side of the chimney to remain, instead of those two sign-posts, done by nobody knew who, that had been removed to make way for them. To which the King answered, "My Lord, I have a great respect for your taste in what you understand, but in pictures I beg leave to follow my own. I suppose you assisted the Queen with your fine advice when she was pulling my house to pieces and spoiling all my furniture. Thank God, at least she has left the walls standing! As for the Vandykes, I do not care whether they are changed or no; but for the picture with the dirty frame over the door, and the three nasty little children, I will have them taken away, and the old ones restored; I will have it done too to-morrow morning before I go to London, or else I know it will not be done at all." "Would your Majesty," said Lord

Hervey, "have the gigantic fat Venus restored too?" "Yes, my lord; I am not so nice as your Lordship. I like my fat Venus much better than anything you have given me instead of her." Lord Hervey thought, though he did not dare to say, that, if His Majesty had liked his fat Venus as well as he used to do, there would have been none of these disputations. . . .'

Hervey's heart fell when he heard all this, because he knew the frames of the removed pictures had been altered for their successors, that the 'fat Venus' was at Windsor and some of the other pictures at Hampton Court. The 'three nasty little children' were probably Charles I's children, now at Windsor, by Van Dyck. When Hervey told the Queen, she 'affected to laugh, but was a good deal displeased, and more ashamed. . . . Whilst they were speaking the King came in, but, by good luck, said not one word of the pictures. His Majesty stayed about five minutes in the gallery; snubbed the Queen, who was drinking chocolate, for being always stuffing, the Princess Emily for not hearing him, the Princess Caroline for being grown fat, the Duke for standing awkwardly, Lord Hervey for not knowing what relation the Prince of Sultzbach was to the Elector Palatine, and then carried the Queen to walk, and be resnubbed, in the garden.' But the pictures had to be changed, Hervey making an excuse for the delay.

Although the Queen was balked on this occasion, she had achieved an unchallengeable success in 1728 when she had rediscovered in an old bureau at Kensington some of the finest drawings in the Royal Collection, including about a hundred of Holbein's sketches. Some of these she hung in her own closet at Kensington, which became a crowded and delightful picture gallery, of which she was proud.

The Queen anticipated the Victorian convention of ignoring 'the other woman'; in so doing, she ran the risk of being accused of pandering to the King's desires, for in his long rambling affectionate letters he told her in great detail of all his romantic ambitions. Some of Hervey's stories are so absurd as to be almost incredible. George once got it into his head that he would like to have an affair with the Princess of Modena, whom he had never seen, and begged 'ma chère Caroline' to assist in bringing it about. It was easy for the Queen to ignore such an undignified plea in a letter of forty pages; but her relationship with Mrs Howard (later Lady Suffolk), one of her 'women of the bedchamber' who was also welcome in George's bedchamber, proved necessarily more complicated. She firmly refused to be blackmailed into paying £1,200 a year 'to Mr Howard to let his wife stay with me'. But, she told Hervey, 'after all this matter was settled, the first thing this wise, prudent Lady Suffolk did was to pick a quarrel with me about holding a basin in the ceremony of my dressing, and to tell me, with her little fierce eyes, and cheeks as red as your coat, that positively she would not do it; to which I made her no answer then in anger, but calmly, as I would have said to a naughty child: 'Yes, my dear Howard, I am sure you will; indeed you will. Go, go! fie for shame!" . . .'

Hervey wrote a little playlet for the Queen's amusement. It has a scene in the Queen's dressing-room, where she is discovered cleaning her teeth. Morning prayers are being said in the next room:

> '1 PARSON (*behind the scenes*): "From pride, vain glory, and hypocrisy, from envy, hatred, and malice, and all uncharitableness."
>
> 2 PARSON: "Good Lord deliver us!"
>
> QUEEN: "I pray, my good Lady Sundon, shut a little that door: those creatures pray so loud, one cannot hear oneself speak. (LADY SUNDON *goes to shut the door*.) So, so, not quite so much; leave it enough open for those parsons to think we may hear, and enough shut that we may not hear quite so much. . . ."'

To have a Boswell at court may be a posthumous embarrass-
ment to royalty, but is undoubtedly a blessing to historians.
Thanks to Hervey, the daily life of this fantastic court has been
fully revealed – and never more thoroughly than in the
numerous stories about the Prince of Wales. In 1736, when
there was some doubt as to whether the Princess was likely to
be pregnant, Hervey reports an amazing Shakespearian
conversation with the Queen, as to whether he 'could contrive,
if he and you were both willing, without her knowledge to go
to bed to her instead of him?' 'Nothing so easy,' replied
Hervey, and he proceeded to indicate how he would do it.
A less startling subject of discussion was the behaviour of the
Prince and his wife at chapel. 'The Prince and Princess, whether
from an air of grandeur or by chance I know not, used generally to come to chapel at Kensington after the service had been
some time begun.' The Queen was annoyed when the Princess
passed before her, 'between the Queen and where her book
lay'; but the Prince was so obstinate that he simply ordered
the Princess not to go to chapel at all.

The last illness and death of the Queen at St James's in
November, 1737, forms the climax of Hervey's Memoirs,
and even Hervey's starkly clinical account cannot disguise the
tenderness he felt for the friend who had done so much for
him. When the Queen was first taken ill, of what was thought
to be colic, she was dosed with a desperate collection of
remedies, among them 'Daffy's Elixir', mint-water, usque-
baugh (whisky), snake-root, and 'Sir Walter Raleigh's cordial'.
Having been 'blooded', she seemed better, and the King
sufficiently overcame his concern to make sure that new
ruffles were sewn on to his shirt. But to Hervey, who was

continually with her, the Queen confessed: 'I have an ill which nobody knows of.' She grew worse again, and the King then told a surgeon that she had a long-standing rupture which she had been absolutely determined to ignore. An immediate operation was undertaken, but it was too late to save her.

The Queen spoke bitterly of the Prince of Wales: 'At least I shall have one comfort in having my eyes eternally closed – I shall never see that monster again.' Taking off a ruby ring that the King had given her at her coronation, she put it on his finger and said: 'This is the last thing I have to give you – naked I came to you, and naked I go from you. I had everything I ever possessed from you, and to you whatever I have I return. My will you will find a very short one; I give all I have to you.'

She had always wished that the King should marry again, and now she repeated her wish. The King was deeply moved:

'. . . His sobs began to rise and his tears to fall with double vehemence. Whilst in the midst of this passion, wiping his eyes, and sobbing between every word, with much ado he got out this answer: "Non – j'aurai – des – maîtresses." To which the Queen made no other reply than: "Ah! mon Dieu! cela n'empêche pas." '

Hervey adds: 'I know this episode will hardly be credited, but it is literally true.'

She then said she felt she could sleep. 'The King said many kind things to her and kissed her face and her hands a hundred times.' But when she asked for her watch which hung by the chimney, in order that he could take care of her seal, his temper suddenly flared out again. 'Ah! my God! let it alone; the Queen has always such strange fancies. Who should meddle with your seal? Is it not as safe there as in my pocket?'

The Queen lingered until 20 November, by which time the

King was overwhelmed with grief, and the whole family were utterly exhausted. The King spoke continually 'of the Queen's good qualities, his fondness for her, his anxiety for her welfare, and the irreparable loss her death would be to him'. Of all his sayings, perhaps the following best expresses the essential truth about Queen Caroline: 'Poor woman, how she always found something obliging, agreeable, and pleasing to say to everybody, and always sent people away from her better satisfied than they came! *Comme elle soutenoit sa dignité avec grace, avec politesse, avec douceur!*'

7 · THE ROYAL WIDOWER

The author of a eulogistic essay on Queen Caroline, published soon after her death, devoted a respectfully long-winded paragraph to her bereaved husband:

> 'If I was at liberty to go into more particulars, and describe the pains and anxiety of his Royal Breast, so visible in his whole conduct, whilst All that He loved, and valued was in danger; the distraction of thought; the oppression of heart; and the deluge of soft and tender passions, that broke in upon a mind, naturally fortified with the utmost degree of constancy and resolution; while He appeared himself to feel all the agonies of death, when the last glimmering of hope was gone: If it were possible for all this to be freely and fully described, it would be a stronger motive than any that has yet been urged, to engage the most affectionate wishes and prayers of his subjects, for the preservation of a PRINCE who has added to his confessed virtues of inflexible Probity, Justice, Honor and Truth, the most amiable proofs of his Humanity, Tenderness and Goodness of heart.'

Boiled down, this paragraph means that the King's evident and genuine grief induced general sympathy, and made him, in Hervey's less flowery language, 'for some time more popular and better spoken of than he had ever been before this incident, or than I believe he ever will be again'. Hervey described the King, during his seclusion after his wife's death, as talking incessantly of her, of himself, and of his relations. In anxiety for his master's health, Sir Robert Walpole was concerned to restore the King to the arms of an old mistress, Lady Deloraine. This was duly achieved. The King did not marry again.

Hervey brought his Memoirs to a close with the death of the Queen. The King was glad to have him with him in his distress, but Hervey told Sir Robert Walpole that he had 'long made it my sole business to please the Queen and you', and took the opportunity of asking for political preferment. Though the response was not immediate, in 1739 Hervey was appointed Lord Privy Seal. An unfamiliar but attractive portrait by Thomas Hudson shows him holding the bag that symbolizes his office (Plate IV). He had not long to enjoy his promotion, however, and he died in 1743. For the remainder of the reign, an historian feels the absence of this diverting chronicler, for whom Horace Walpole (Plate IV) becomes the nearest substitute.

Horace's house, Strawberry Hill, Twickenham, was itself a decorative creation. He himself was typical of those busy bachelors, men of humour, taste and fashion with a wide social acquaintance, connoisseurs of art and *virtu*, who play such a large part in the cultivated life of their times.

A gifted, prolific author, he not only invented the Gothic novel and produced the *Memoirs of the Reign of King George the Second*, but also wrote innumerable brilliant letters, which are highly entertaining and have won him lasting fame. Though he lacked Hervey's intimate acquaintance with the royal family, Horace Walpole was a chronicler who illuminated the history of the court – more especially in his letters; the Memoirs are largely political, as befitted a man of some unsatisfied political ambition and the youngest son of Sir Robert Walpole.

He had much in common with John, Lord Hervey, including poor health, a predilection for witty, scandalous gossip, and a certain inbred preciosity and affectation; his morals were sounder, his good nature more evident. It was often hinted that the connection between Hervey and Horace Walpole was closer than appeared, and that he was actually not the son of Sir Robert Walpole but of Carr, Lord Hervey, the elder brother of the diarist. Certainly, Horace was born (in 1717) eleven years after the birth of the preceding child of

Sir Robert and his wife, whose marriage latterly was far from happy; and certainly, again, Horace was in many respects more of a Hervey than a Walpole. But the theory remains an intriguing, though plausible speculation; Horace was devoted to his mother; and he showed, in Peter Cunningham's words, 'the utmost unbounded filial regard' for Sir Robert Walpole.

The latter remained Prime Minister for five years after the death of his staunch friend Queen Caroline. Sir Robert Walpole had given England twenty years of peace, and he owed his downfall in 1742 to being drawn into an unsuccessful war with Spain. The 'War of Jenkins' Ear' resulted partly from the indignation aroused by the mutilation of Captain Jenkins by Spanish Custom-house officials (he preserved his ear in a box and showed it to the House of Commons), and partly from the bellicosity of the King. Robustly cynical as usual, Walpole endeavoured to soothe the King's restlessness by bringing over from Hanover his old mistress, Amelia Sophia Marianne von Walmoden. In the spirit of the notorious conversation at his wife's deathbed, George established her at court and created her Countess of Yarmouth, but in public affairs he neither invited nor accepted her advice, nor did he pamper her in private. The rivalry between Lady Yarmouth and Lady Deloraine had a comical ending. Horace Walpole wrote to Sir Horace Mann on 8 October 1742:

> 'There has been a great fracas at Kensington; one of the Mesdames [George II's daughters] pulled the chair from under Countess Deloraine at cards, who, being provoked that her Monarch was diverted with her disgrace, with the malice of a hobby-horse, gave him just such another fall. But alas! the Monarch, like Louis

XIV, is mortal in the part that touched the ground, and was so hurt and so angry, that the Countess is disgraced, and her German rival [Lady Yarmouth] remains in the sole and quiet possession of her royal master's favour.'

As a consequence of the Spanish war, England was again involved in war with France. For the last time an English King commanded his troops in the field. George led his army to victory at Dettingen in 1743 and behaved with great gallantry. 'The King was in all the heat of the fire, and safe,' wrote Horace Walpole to Mann. '. . . How happy it is that the King has had such an opportunity of distinguishing himself! What a figure he will make!' The royal example advanced his popularity at home, and his cry – 'Now, boys, for the honour of England; fire, and behave bravely and the French will soon run' – was remembered by the ordinary soldier. He received a tremendous welcome when he returned to London: 'They almost carried him into the palace on their shoulders,' wrote Horace Walpole, 'and at night the whole town was illuminated and bonfired.'

This resurgence of loyalty was timely, for Jacobite hopes were revived by the French war. The King faced the threat of 'the Forty-five' with remarkable calmness. 'When the Ministers propose any thing with regard to the Rebellion, he cries, "Pho! don't talk to me of that stuff", ' wrote Horace Walpole to Mann (13 September 1745). And later, in the punishment of the rebels, the King was inclined to be merciful, unlike his son the Duke of Cumberland.

The continental war went better by sea than by land, so that in May 1749 the country celebrated peace with relief. Lady Yarmouth persuaded the King to order 'a jubilee-masquerade' at Ranelagh. 'Nothing in a fairy tale ever surpassed it,' declared Horace Walpole. A few days later there was a 'subscription-masquerade'; Walpole reported that 'the

King was well disguised in an old-fashioned English habit, and much pleased with somebody who desired him to hold their cup as they were drinking tea'.

During the next seven years England enjoyed an uneasy calm under the rule of Henry Pelham and his brother the Duke of Newcastle, a period which culminated in 1756 in the Seven Years War and world-wide British conquests. But for the time being there was leisure to contemplate domestic difficulties and renewed allegations of dampness at Kensington Palace. On 17 August 1749 Horace Walpole wrote to Mann:

'There is nothing like news: Kensington Palace had like to have made an article the other night; it was on fire: my Lady Yarmouth has an ague, and is forced to keep a constant fire in her room against the damps. When my Lady Suffolk lived in that apartment, the floor produced a constant crop of mushrooms. Though there are so many vacant chambers, the King hoards all he can, and has locked up half the palace since the Queen's death: so he does at St James's, and I believe would put the rooms out to interest, if he could get a closet a year for them! Somebody told my Lady Yarmouth they wondered she would live in that unwholesome apartment, when there are so many other rooms: she replied, "Mais pas pour moy".'

The apartment may have been that originally occupied by George I's mistress, the Duchess of Kendal.

The death of the Prince of Wales in 1751 left his son George (later George III) as heir to the throne; and the doggerel epitaph beginning

> Here lies Fred,
> Who was alive and is dead.
> Had it been his father,
> I had much rather . . .

suggests that the King, and indeed the whole royal family, were again out of favour. The King was growing sensitive to his age: in November 1751, according to Walpole, he watched a farce at Drury Lane in which one character told another, 'You are villainously old; you are sixty-six; you can't have the impudence to think of living above two years.' At which the King in the stage-box remarked: 'This is d——d stuff!'

The feeling grew that the Whigs, who were committed to the King's German interests, had outlasted their time; Lady Yarmouth's attempt to act as William Pitt's intermediary was met by the King with the rebuff that she 'does not meddle and shall not meddle'; but the renewal of war with France compelled George to accept Pitt, who said truly: 'I know that I can save this country and that no one else can.' Paradoxically, Pitt's revival of patriotism under the new Tory party brought the old King much esteem during his last years. His faults were now forgotten in his positive good qualities. He continued to play his part with his accustomed courage; catching cold on coming to town from Kensington in November 1758, he became seriously ill, but struggled out of bed on a cold day to appear at court, earning Pitt's praise and general loyalty and affection. His reward was that 'year of victories', 1759: the capture of Quebec, the triumphs of Quiberon and Minden, Clive's consolidation of his successes in India.

In May 1760 Horace Walpole mentions that, though the spring was 'far from warm', the King 'wears a silk coat and has left off fires'. His death at Kensington Palace, on 25 October 1760, was sudden. Horace Walpole had not been to court for ten years, but, as luck would have it, had arranged to present himself and to kiss hands on the following day. Walpole reported the news to George Montagu within a few hours:

'He went to bed well last night, rose at six this morning as usual, looked, I suppose, if all his money was in his purse, and called for his chocolate. A little after seven, he went into the water-closet; the German *valet de chambre* heard a noise, listened, heard something like a groan, ran in, and found the hero of Oudenarde and Dettingen on the floor, with a gash on his right temple, by falling against the corner of a bureau. He tried to speak, could not, and expired. . . .'

The King had died in a small room between the lavatory and his bedroom. Walpole continued his letter to Montagu: 'He probably got his death, as he liked to have done two years ago, by viewing the troops for the expedition from the wall of Kensington Garden. My Lady Suffolk told me about a month ago that he had often told her, speaking of the dampness of Kensington, that he would never die there.'

In another letter to Montagu, of 28 October, Walpole permitted himself some reflections on the human comedy and the ephemeral nature of fame:

'P.S. I smiled to myself last night. Out of excess of attention, which costs me nothing, when I mean it should cost nobody else anything, I went last night to Kensington to inquire after Princess Emily and Lady Yarmouth: nobody knew me, they asked my name. When they heard it, they did not seem ever to have heard it before, even in that house. I waited half an hour in a lodge with a footman of Lady Yarmouth's; I would not have waited so long in her room a week ago; now it only diverted me. Even moralizing is entertaining, when one laughs at the same time; but I pity those who don't moralize till they cry.'

Seen through Walpole's eyes, the funeral at Westminster Abbey had richly comic aspects. The Duke of Newcastle was affected almost to hysteria and had to be treated by the Archbishop with a smelling bottle; and he had such a fear of

Drawings of Augustus Frederick, Duke of Sussex.
by Sir Francis Chantrey (see p. 66).

Library of the Duke of Sussex Kensington Palace

Drawing of the Duke of Sussex
in his library at Kensington
Palace, 1826.
By George Cruikshank
(see p. 67).

PLATE VII

Edward, Duke of Kent, 1818. Oil painting by Sir William Beechey (see p. 72).

The Duchess of Kent, 1829. Miniature by Sir William Ross (See p. 76).

PLATE VIII

catching cold that 'the Duke of Cumberland, who was sinking with heat, felt himself weighed down, and turning round, found it was the Duke of Newcastle standing upon his train, to avoid the chill of the marble'. The King was laid beside Queen Caroline, and, by his wish, the adjacent sides of their coffins were removed, so that there should be no barrier between them – a final comment on Lady Suffolk, Lady Yarmouth and a good many more.

The new King, George III, had Kensington memories of his first love Lady Sarah Lennox, who as a child of four or five had greeted his grandfather on the Broad Walk with 'Comment vous portez-vous, Monsieur le Roi? Vous avez une grande et belle maison ici, n'est-ce-pas?' George II was disappointed by her shyness when he saw her again at the age of fourteen, but the Prince of Wales was captivated by her, and might indeed have married her on his accession, if she had been old enough to take her opportunity, and if his mother had not married him off to Princess Charlotte of Mecklenburg.

But George III had no wish to reside at Kensington Palace. As early as 1756, Horace Walpole said that he 'desired to be excused living at Kensington'. In fact, no English monarch lived there again until the young Queen Victoria; and she did so only for a short time.

For seventy years, however, the Palace had been at the centre of the life and government of the kingdom. The strongest memories are those of the longest inhabitant George II and his Queen, and we are chiefly indebted to Lord Hervey and to Horace Walpole for keeping them alive in their Kensington setting. They in turn are revived for us in the portraits by Thomas Hudson and his pupil Joshua Reynolds

(Plate IV). Reynolds's masterly impression of Walpole emphasizes the distance between Reynolds and his old teacher, yet Hudson's portrait of Hervey is pleasing enough to suggest that he has been somewhat unjustly overshadowed. And, in studying them, it is hard to resist the conclusion that we are looking at portraits of an uncle and his nephew.

8 · TWO DUKES AND A REJECTED QUEEN

After the death of George II, the State Rooms of Kensington Palace were closed, and for about forty years the rest of the Palace stood largely empty, though it appears that a number of residents, including the Dowager Duchess of Manchester, had to move out to make room for the Princess of Wales in 1808. The neglect of the interior means that it contains no work by Adam, but the State Rooms were kept in good order. The Broad Walk remained a fashionable promenade. The domestic gardens were maintained. In 1784 William Forsyth was appointed King's Gardener at Kensington. He was an authority on fruit trees, who devoted himself especially to fruit and vegetables, the Kensington garden becoming one of the chief suppliers of the Royal Household. Forsyth was a founder of the Royal Horticultural Society, and is commemorated by the genus *Forsythia* of spring flowering shrubs.

At the beginning of the nineteenth century the Palace stirred from slumber; it again acquired royal residents, and with them a richly diversified social life. By 1808 a new chaplain had been appointed for their benefit; the Lord Chamberlain's Accounts show that by 1811 the chapel had been hopefully refurnished with 'Scarlet Cushions, Curtains, &c, complete' (P.R.O.).

George III's ill-starred niece and daughter-in-law Caroline, Princess of Wales, lived at the Palace from 1808 to 1814, and so for a time did her mother. By 1820 George III's daughter, the fragile and increasingly blind Princess Sophia (Plate IX), was a resident. But the Palace became particularly associated with the fourth and sixth sons of George III, Edward Augustus, Duke of Kent, and Augustus Frederick,

Duke of Sussex. Although the period of residence of the Duke of Kent was to prove in the long run the more important, that of the Duke of Sussex was the longer, and it will be convenient to deal with it first.

Prince Augustus, later Duke of Sussex (Plate VII), born in 1773, was in many ways the most likeable, intelligent and congenial of the notorious royal Dukes. He was tall and largely built; a life-long warm-hearted Whig; a great collector and reader of books. It must be admitted that he suffered from vanity, as well as asthma, being especially proud of his singing voice, which he claimed spanned three octaves, while his generous temper led him not only into political controversy but also into a romantic entanglement which disturbed the course of his life. As a youth of twenty, he fell desperately in love, in Rome, with Lady Augusta Murray, who was considerably older than himself. Although he realized that he had no hope of obtaining his father's consent to his union with a lady who was not of royal birth, he insisted on being married to her in Rome by an English clergyman. They were remarried in December 1793, at St George's, Hanover Square. Both marriages having been officially annulled, the Prince found it convenient to live abroad with his 'wife'; the English climate was anyway bad for his asthma.

By 1801 the romance had run its course. The Prince then settled for a parliamentary grant of £12,000 a year (later raised to £18,000) and the titles Duke of Sussex, Earl of Inverness and Baron of Arklow. Henceforth, he and Lady Augusta lived apart, while their two children, who were given the name d'Este, lived with their father.

From 1806 the Duke of Sussex and his large library were

housed in Kensington Palace. He was not unduly extravagant, and bookcases are perhaps the most conspicuous items debited to him in the Lord Chamberlain's Accounts. The Duke was lodged in the southern range of Clock Court; his fifty thousand books filled the Long Gallery on the first floor (Plate VII); the unique collection of biblical manuscripts and the five thousand Bibles occupied a special Divinity Room. Wren's entrance to the Palace from the portico on Palace Green through the Stone Gallery to the King's Staircase was no longer used. The double doors at the end of the Stone Gallery were sealed; the opening from the Guard Room to the staircase was closed, and the Guard Room was divided horizontally by the insertion of a floor. These measures suggest that it was thought unlikely that the Palace would again be employed as the monarch's residence; the alterations were not irreversible, but they remained permanent.

The Duke's progressive views often brought him into collision with his elder brother, the Prince of Wales, and when the latter became King in 1820 the Duke took the side of his estranged consort, Queen Caroline, who had been his neighbour in Kensington Palace. Visiting Battle Abbey in 1820, the Duke was greeted by cries of 'The Queen and Sussex for ever'.

Not surprisingly, the quarrel with George IV grew bitter; but there was a death-bed reconciliation, after the Duke had sent his brother a huge invalid chair which had been made for him when he could not lie down at night because of his asthma.

The Duke had actually been mysteriously cured of asthma, the complaint which so often figures in the history of Kensington Palace; but he had serious trouble with his eyesight (involving the use of fifteen pairs of spectacles) and worried continually over his health. He was a keen gardener, and very fond of singing birds, and of watches and clocks, which interrupted his conversation with visitors when they struck.

This bold and eloquent politician had the right to feel a personal pride in the passing of the Reform Bill of 1832, for he had played a considerable part in the triumph. Towards the end of his life he was a well-loved figure throughout the country. He had long been associated with philanthropic and charitable causes. He was President of the Society of Arts for twenty-seven years, and there is a very pleasant description of him presenting a silver medal for drawing to the nine-year-old John Millais in 1839. He failed to see the boy at first because his curly head did not appear over the top of the desk, but the Duke got up and gave him a stool to stand on. The Duke could not make much of the prize drawing, though he tried various pairs of glasses; however, he patted young Millais on the head and asked him to let him know if he could ever do anything to help him. John Millais and his brother turned this promise to good account when they had difficulty in obtaining the special tickets they required to fish in the Serpentine and Round Pond.

The later years of the agreeable eccentric Duke were made happy, after the death of his first wife, by his marriage to the widowed Lady Cecilia Buggin. This marriage was as illegal as the other, but Queen Victoria, who was very fond of her uncle, softened the blow by creating Lady Cecilia, Duchess of Inverness, to correspond with one of the Duke's titles. He maintained his suite at Kensington, but he and his Duchess also had a small house overlooking Hyde Park. Queen Victoria drove specially to Kensington Palace to see her uncle, shortly before he died on 21 April 1843. A good man, certainly, who despite all those Bibles declared that he didn't 'believe a word' of the Athanasian Creed.

In his will the Duke directed that surgeons should undertake a post mortem on his body for 'the good of my fellow men'. He was buried, by his own wish, in the public cemetery at Kensal Green. His widow, the Duchess of Inverness, lived on in his rooms at Kensington Palace until her death in 1873.

The volatile Princess of Wales made an incongruous figure in Wren's red-brick palace. Caroline Amelia Elizabeth, second daughter of Duke Charles of Brunswick–Wolfenbüttel and George III's sister, Princess Augusta, was born in 1768 and grew up an attractive, lively, flirtatious, intelligent girl; she was also obstinate, self-willed and more than a little indiscreet and tactless. But it was a harsh fate that in 1795 joined this wayward and vulnerable character in marriage with her cousin George, Prince of Wales. Like his brother the Duke of Sussex, the Prince had already contracted an illegal marriage with Mrs Fitzherbert; his marriage with Caroline was purely one of convenience, designed to provide the throne with an heir. Moreover, he had other mistresses, notably Lady Jersey, who connived at a marriage that would leave her in a dominating position.

Caroline held no illusions about the marriage, but the reality was worse than she had anticipated. Mystery surrounds the wedding night, and there have been suggestions that Caroline's daughter, Princess Charlotte, born in 1796, was not the Prince's child. Certainly, Caroline detested her dissipated husband at sight, while the Prince was revolted by her brash manners, which may partly be attributed to a pathetic bravado in desperate circumstances. Caroline received the sympathy of her father-in-law and of most of her brothers-in-law, but separation from her husband came swiftly and irrevocably. Before long she was living at Blackheath, and in 1801 moved to

Montague House there. She consoled herself with male company, and suspicion was aroused that a small boy, William Austin, whom she took into her household, was her bastard son. A commission appointed to investigate her conduct – it was called 'the Delicate Investigation' – acquitted Caroline on the main charge, but could not deny that her general conduct gave scope for 'very unfavourable interpretations'.

But popular sympathy for Caroline had never been lacking, and was used as political capital by Tories and Whigs in turn. In 1807 the King again received the Princess of Wales at court and granted her apartments in Kensington Palace. Bringing William Austin with her, she arrived there in June 1808 and spent most of the next six years at Kensington. Her rooms were lavishly equipped; she slept in a 'double headed Couch Bedstead, carv'd heads & Paws, finished in Burnished Gold', which cost £106 10s. 0d., according to the Lord Chamberlain's Accounts (P.R.O.).

Caroline shocked the conventional inhabitants of Kensington by her eccentric but initially harmless behaviour. At first many distinguished guests accepted her invitations, ranging from Scott to Byron and from Lord Eldon to Spencer Perceval. She showed charm and gaiety, but dressed exotically and wore too much rouge; indeed, she was odd, perhaps a little crazy. In Kensington Gardens, a prim place in those days, she walked hatless and talked on a bench to strangers. Most irresponsible! Things grew worse after her husband became Regent in 1811, when he made it clear that his wife's visitors would not be received at Carlton House. Caroline felt more than ever spurned, and began to take an interest in a family of Italian musicians called Sapio. Rumours that the handsome young Sapio was her lover increased when she rented two adjoining cottages in Bayswater, installed the Sapios in one of them, and visited them after dinner in the evening. With the Tories supporting the Prince Regent, Caroline was henceforth to be championed by the Whigs; they persuaded her to send the Sapios to live elsewhere.

There was plenty of further scandal. Caroline's daughter, Princess Charlotte, had hitherto visited her mother at Kensington twice a week; the Prince Regent now insisted that his consent must be obtained for each visit. He distrusted Caroline's influence on her daughter, with some reason, for it later appeared that she had connived at an affair between the girl and one Captain Hesse; according to Charlotte, she once actually locked the couple into her own bedroom at Kensington, with some provocative remarks. The conduct of Caroline thus takes a more sinister turn; in the light of her daughter's statement, one can believe almost anything of her.

In this situation, it appeared desirable to the Prince Regent that Charlotte should be married. The choice fell on the Prince of Orange; he was quite a personable young man, and Charlotte allowed herself to become engaged; but there were two snags: first, the Prince was a drunkard, and, secondly the marriage with him would mean living temporarily in Holland. Charlotte broke off the engagement, and took refuge at her mother's house in Connaught Square, whence she was extricated by the good offices of the Duke of Sussex and returned to Carlton House. Her marriage to Prince Leopold of Saxe-Coburg in 1816 seemed likely to be more successful, but came to a tragic end with her death in childbirth in the following year.

By then the Princess of Wales had left Kensington for the Continent, where her loose behaviour provided scandalous evidence during the hearing of a Bill of Divorce against her in the House of Lords in 1820. Although the Bill was abandoned, Queen Caroline was refused admittance to her husband's coronation, and died dispirited in 1821 – still the favourite of the people, as she had always been. The residence of this Bohemian eccentric contributes a bizarre episode to the history of Kensington Palace.

It is time to turn to someone more conventional, though scarcely more fortunate. The connection of Edward, Duke of Kent (Plate VIII), with Kensington Palace began in 1799, when he was granted apartments which at first he found 'so comfortless as to be almost uninhabitable'. He was then thirty-two, having been born on 2 November 1767. He had been born into an atmosphere of gloom, for his arrival coincided with the death of his father's favourite brother, Edward, Duke of York, after whom he was named. Following a pleasant childhood at Kew, he was sent at seventeen to Lüneburg in Germany to be trained as a soldier. There he accepted the principles of stern discipline which were to characterize his professional life.

He was a man who always went to extremes. His abstemiousness, punctuality and early rising did not prevent him becoming a martinet or acquiring habits of great extravagance; so that his character, at least until later life, was a mixture of the admirable and deplorable. It must be added, however, that he was treated casually by his father and did not receive his parliamentary grant of £12,000 a year until he was thirty-one, when he was saddled with enormous debts.

By this time he had already shown his gifts and limitations as a soldier. From Lüneburg he had gone to Geneva, where his social activities had proved extremely costly. In 1790 he was sent to Gibraltar as Colonel of the Royal Fusiliers; there he made himself so unpopular that he was ordered with his regiment to North America; before he left the Rock he gave himself a luxurious banquet (he had a liking for ceremonial music, and fifty musicians played in his honour). In Canada he did better; the troops were provoked almost to mutiny by his sadistic severity, but the civilian population approved his efforts to forward the claims of music, Freemasonry, and education; to the public at large he had the right conciliatory approach, telling French Canadians who had rioted after an election: 'You are all His Britannic Majesty's beloved Canadian subjects.' Another popular move was to choose as his mistress the French Canadian Madame Julie de St Laurent, with whom he lived on terms of mutual devotion for nearly thirty years. He also maintained intimate and affectionate relations with a French Canadian family, the de Salaberrys.

In 1793, promoted major-general, the Duke increased his reputation by a successful campaign against the French islands of the West Indies. He returned to Canada as commander of the British troops in Nova Scotia, and in 1799 he became commander-in-chief of the forces in British North America. This did not prevent him taking extended leave in England, where he settled nominally at Kensington but actually with *Madame* in Knightsbridge. His next official appointment was, in all the circumstances, astonishing; not surprisingly, it proved to be his last.

The Gibraltar garrison had grown so indisciplined that the Government looked for a man with an iron hand; in 1802 the Duke was appointed Governor-General. Feeling no sympathy for the tedium of service on the Rock, he closed fifty wine shops and issued a list of orders which virtually segregated sergeants from corporals and corporals from privates; he insisted that officers' hair must be cut once a month, that the men should not grow whiskers, and more to the same effect. This time, as Belloc might have said in another cautionary tale, mutiny 'did break out'. The 25th Regiment attacked the Duke's regiment, the Royals. The trouble was quelled with floggings and three death sentences, but the

73

Duke was recalled. He returned to England absolutely furious, blaming what he considered his unfair treatment on his brother, the Duke of York.

The Duke of Kent lived for many years under a cloud. He was promoted field marshal and his income was raised to £18,000, but he had nothing to do, and his debts amounted to £200,000. He became involved in scandalous quarrels with the Duke of York and the Prince of Wales. He made over much of his income to his creditors, and retired temporarily to Brussels, but soon came back again. Meanwhile, between 1806 and 1814, he had paid £13,000 to remodel his apartments at Kensington Palace, where he had a special bedroom fitted up for his friend Louis Philippe. It was at this time that the *porte cochère* and entrance hall from Clock Court was added, with a hall beyond, from which an elegant double staircase ascends to the present entrance to the London Museum. Page after page of entries in the Lord Chamberlain's Accounts testify that the Duke's extravagance was, alas, no fiction. Even so, he continued to spend most of his time at his house in Knightsbridge. His godson Edward de Salaberry, aged fifteen, indicated the situation in a letter to his father of 30 December 1807: 'I am at present staying with H.R.H. the Duke of Kent at Kensington Palace, where I have fine apartments. H.R.H. and Madame de St Laurent are at present at Knightsbridge which is some distance from here. It is a superb mansion beautifully furnished. . . .'

He had a country house, too, at Castle Hill Lodge, Ealing, and his biographer Erskine Neale affords 'a peep at the Duke in private life' there, in 1811, from the pen of Mr Justice Hardinge. The Judge was received by a porter in livery, then by the head gardener 'in his best clothes', and finally by the house-steward and six footmen, who passed him on to a valet. It appeared that the Duke periodically inspected the dress and cleanliness of his servants with military precision.

At breakfast a band of thirty wind-instruments, hidden behind a glass door, played a dirge, in memory of the visitor's sailor son, so affectingly that the Judge wept. The Duke took his hand, saying, 'Those are tears which do none of us any harm!'

The Duke regulated his life by pulling bells. According to Neale, he had five separate pulls at Kensington Palace, with gilt handles, 'conspicuously placed in a small alcove in the parlour, next Kensington gardens, for the purpose of summoning an equal number of domestics'. Like the Duke of Sussex, he loved chiming clocks. His punctuality was fanatical, and if you had the misfortune to arrive ten minutes late, you would be greeted with: 'I thought I should not have had the pleasure of seeing you today.'

Clearly the Duke, alternating between severity and extravagant kindliness, was something of a Jekyll and Hyde. But as he grew older, and realized perhaps that Prussian discipline was not a universal panacea, his good qualities came to predominate in public as they always had done in private. In 1816 he presided at seventy-two charity meetings. The Literary Fund interested him particularly; he told a correspondent in 1815: 'England, who has Chelsea and Greenwich for her decayed soldiers and sailors, might with propriety provide some peaceful asylum for the aged and worn-out writer, when the power to think and the ability to record fail (as they must inevitably do) eventually, from the pressure of years and unremitting exertion.' The British and Foreign School Society, another cause that he favoured, held committee meetings at Kensington Palace under his chairmanship.

The unexpected death of Princess Charlotte in 1817 reopened the question of the future succession to the throne. This faced the Duke with a painful decision. The sons of George III had been singularly unsuccessful in producing legitimate heirs. While looking through the newspaper at breakfast in Brussels one morning, Madame de St Laurent fainted when she read that it had become essential that the Duke of Kent should marry. 'God only knows the sacrifice it will be to make,' the Duke told Creevey. 'It is now seven and twenty years that Madame St Laurent and I have lived together. . . .' It was a call to patriotic duty indeed, but he quickly made up his mind and soon found a suitable bride; he had, in fact, had his eye on her for some time. She was the widowed Princess Victoria of Leiningen, sister of Prince Leopold, short, plump, cheerful, healthy and talkative (Plate VIII); there were worse prospects. The couple were married in 1818, and Madame de St Laurent retired sadly into a convent. The English public was, not unnaturally, rather amused, but it was not so funny for the Duke and his Julie.

The Duke began his married life at his wife's home at Amorbach in Germany. However, when it was known that she was pregnant, he determined that they must return to England for the birth of their child. Money was so short, and assistance so tardy, that the Duke himself drove the coach. In April 1819 they were installed in the rooms under the State apartments on the east side of Kensington Palace – rooms once occupied by the Princess of Wales – and on 24 May 1819 a daughter was born in the room at the north-east corner, which had only been completely decorated two days before.*

On 24 June, in the Cupola Room above, the Archbishop of Canterbury christened her Alexandrina, after her godfather

---

*At 10 p.m. on 24 May, the Duke of Kent wrote to the Dowager Duchess of Saxe-Coburg: 'Je commence ma lettre par vous annoncer que notre chère petite Victoire est accouchée ce matin à 4 heures et quart, ici dans le vieux Palais de nos Ancêtres, d'une petite fille, qui est vraiment un modèle de force et de beauté, réuni. . . .' (RA. M. 3/3).

the Tsar of Russia, and Victoria after her mother. Her father having originally proposed Georgina as the second name, Victoria was introduced to compose an argument with the Prince Regent. The mother was 'churched' at St Mary Abbots on 29 June, when 'the Duke of Kent led the Duchess to the Communion-table'.

The young Princess was only fifth in line of succession to the throne, but the Duke, surveying his senior brothers, had a mystical belief that the crown would come to him and his children. Later in the year the Duke brought a clerical visitor to the child's cot and responded to his prayer with 'an emphatic Amen'. Then he added: 'Don't pray, simply, that hers may be a brilliant career, and exempt from those trials and struggles which have pursued her father; but pray that God's blessing may rest on her, that it may overshadow her, and that in all her coming years she may be guided and guarded by God.'

The Duke lived only nine months after the birth of his child. He did not at all mind that she was a daughter; he was immensely proud that she was such a healthy infant, and gratified that his wife was able to feed her, assuring a correspondent that the Duchess was 'most happy that the performance of an office, most interesting in its nature, has met with the wishes and feeling of society'. But his financial situation remained much less satisfactory, and he could not see how he and his little family could live in England; he contemplated selling Castle Hill Lodge, Ealing, by a public lottery, but failed to obtain parliamentary sanction; reluctantly planning to return to Amorbach, he decided that they should spend the winter at Sidmouth, Devon, partly for health reasons, partly to avoid his creditors. He died there – a few days before his father, George III – on 23 January 1820, from a neglected cold after getting his feet wet.

The Duke's funeral procession conveying the large coffin

77

proceeded solemnly to Windsor, stopping at Bridport, Blandford, Salisbury and Basingstoke, and meeting mourning crowds everywhere. To many the Duke must have seemed an impecunious failure redeemed by his philanthropy; his little daughter evoked interesting possibilities, but his hasty marriage looked like a sudden postscript to a disappointing life. They could not know that without him nineteenth-century England would have been different, or that, as Roger Fulford has pointed out, 'within a century his descendants were to sit on the thrones of England, Germany, Russia, Norway, Roumania and Spain'. They were denied the exercise of debating how far Queen Victoria's qualities of discipline and patriotism were derived from her controversial soldier father.

Princess Sophia, daughter of
George III.
Miniature by H. Edridge
(see pp. 65 and 82–3).

Sir John Conroy, Bt., 1836.
Miniature by A. Tidey
(see p. 81).

PLATE IX

Princess Victoria in her pony phaeton.
Drawn and engraved by J. Doyle, 1829 (see p. 80).

Princess Victoria in 1836, aged
seventeen.
Miniature by H. Collen.

PLATE X

9 · THE GIRLHOOD OF QUEEN VICTORIA

The Duchess of Kent's brother, the widower Prince Leopold, came to her rescue after the Duke's death, paid the cost of her return journey from Sidmouth with her daughter, and provided an allowance of, first, £2,000 and later £3,000 a year. With this encouragement, she determined to resume her residence at Kensington Palace.

In some reminiscences written in 1872, Queen Victoria described her childhood as 'rather melancholy' and her days with her 'beloved Uncle' at Claremont as the best part of it; but the early childhood, at least, seems to have been happy enough, and she became attached to Kensington Palace. Her first recollections were of crawling on a yellow carpet at Kensington, and of being told that, if she cried and was naughty, her 'Uncle Sussex' would hear her and punish her – 'for which reason I always screamed when I saw him!' She had an early horror of Bishops on account of their wigs and aprons, but she 'partially got over' this when the Bishop of Salisbury (Dr Fisher) knelt down so that she could play with his badge of Chancellor of the Order of the Garter. She enjoyed her visits to Tunbridge Wells, where she usually stayed at Mount Pleasant House (now the Calverley Hotel), and 'the return to Kensington in October or November was generally a day of tears'; her day-nursery with a section of the contemporary wall-paper can still be seen at the hotel. There were also pleasant holidays at Ramsgate and Broadstairs.

The Queen said that she was 'brought up very simply' and 'always slept in my mother's room till I came to the Throne'. Breakfast was at half past eight, luncheon at half past one, dinner at seven – 'to which I came generally (when it was no regular large dinner party) – eating my bread and milk out of a small silver basin.'

When she was five Victoria left the care of her nurse, Mrs Brock ('dear, dear Boppy'), and was put in charge of her governess, Louise Lehzen, daughter of a Lutheran clergyman at Coburg. Fräulein (later Baroness) Lehzen became the chief and best influence on her childhood. It was a strict upbringing, which encouraged the Princess's interest in history, though she had no passion for learning in general; but there was a softer side to the adored Lehzen, for she helped her charge to dress no less than 132 dolls. Victoria's most notable talents were for drawing and music, especially opera and ballet; under expert tuition she became an accomplished amateur artist, while the training of John Sale and Lablache developed a pleasant singing voice. Languages came comparatively easily to her. And thus she grew up, not without a touch of wilfulness, but with a gaiety, a simple piety and a youthful sense of dedication that inspired the devotion of her teachers.

There are many glimpses of Victoria's Kensington youth (Plate X). As early as July 1820, William Wilberforce told Hannah More that he had visited the Duchess and played on the floor with 'her fine animated child'. In August 1822 she was rescued by a soldier in Kensington Gardens when her pony carriage upset. She was often seen, at about the same time, riding a donkey which had been given her by the Duke of York, and offering a friendly greeting to everyone she met. Lord Albemarle watched her, at seven, watering the plants in the Palace garden, wearing a large straw hat and a white cotton dress: 'It was amusing to see how impartially she divided the contents of the watering-pot between the flowers and her own little feet.' Walking along the Broad Walk in 1827, Charles Knight saw her having breakfast on the lawn of the Palace with her mother, and commented on her simplicity and naturalness. A year or so later, Leigh Hunt came upon her in the Gardens walking up a path from the Bayswater Gate, holding the hand of another little girl: 'A magnificent footman in scarlet came behind her, with the splendidest pair of calves in white stockings which we ever beheld.'

She was early aware of her royal dignity, for she once told a child who was about to play with her toys: 'You must not touch those, they are mine; and I may call you Jane, but you must not call me Victoria.' But it was not until March 1830, during a history lesson, that she discovered how close she was to the throne. An extra page had been deliberately inserted into her copy of *Howlett's Tables* of the Kings and Queens of England; it was a genealogical table ending with the names of her Uncles George and William, followed by her own. She wept a little at the discovery and then, raising the forefinger of her right hand, told Lehzen: 'I will be good.'

With her new awareness, the Princess's life changed. In June 1830 the death of George IV made her heir to the throne. Parliament appointed the Duchess of Kent to be Regent in case of need and voted £10,000 a year for the Princess's education. But in the same year 'Uncle Leopold', whose wise advice had hitherto been at the disposal of both mother and child, was invited to become King of the Belgians. This left the Duchess completely under the influence of the Comptroller of her Household, Sir John Conroy (Plate IX). Theirs was a most unfortunate association.

Conroy was an ambitious, unscrupulous intriguer of Anglo-Irish descent, two months older than the Duchess, with ebullient *panache* and a way with women. He had reached the rank of Captain in the army before joining the Duke of Kent's service. His wife, pleasant but weak, failed to realize that her husband was a cad – and dishonest at that. Conroy actually put out a story that, during the latter part of George IV's reign, the Duke of Cumberland was plotting to do away with Victoria – 'All Sir John's invention & Princess Sophia's fearful falseness,' wrote Queen Victoria long afterwards; but it poisoned the atmosphere at Kensington.

Victoria's aunt Sophia (Plate IX) also had Conroy as Comptroller. He dominated her too. Lady Longford quotes a letter written by Princess Sophia to Conroy in October 1830, which shows that she was in league with him in a successful attempt to procure the dismissal of the Duchess's German lady-in-waiting, Baroness Späth. The Baroness resented the way in which Conroy endeavoured to obtain precedence for his wife and daughter, and it was rumoured that she had reproved the Duchess for 'familiarities' with Conroy. But Conroy failed in a similar attempt to oust Lehzen, whom Victoria henceforth increasingly suspected of being a better friend to her than her own mother.

Princess Sophia ended her letter to Conroy: 'God bless you! I hope this is legible. Your *name carefully avoided*. . . .' Conroy flirted with her, as he did with the Duchess, but the liaison was less dangerous; Sophia was over fifty and prematurely aged; her court influence was marginal, though she made a useful spy. This pathetic lady had once been beautiful, a favourite daughter of George III. She had allowed herself to fall in love with his equerry, Colonel Garth, by whom it appears that she had had a child. The episode remains obscure, but it qualified Princess Sophia for a place in Kensington Palace, which had acquired the reputation of a secluded hospital for wayward members of the royal family. There she knitted and spun and embroidered with failing sight, a solitary spirit. Princess Sophia occupied apartments on the first floor in the north-east corner of Clock Court; the Office of Works Papers (P.R.O.) show that at the end of July 1830 her suite was enlarged to include 'Queen Caroline's bed-chamber, dressing-room, water-closet, and little closet' to the east. Enough, perhaps, to confirm her loyalty to Conroy, who would have knowing glances both for her and for the Duchess. In fact, he had both these ladies on a string.

Victoria's references in her diary to her Aunt Sophia are usually formal: 'My aunt Sophia came after dinner' (9 November 1832), or 'Aunt Sophia gave me a dress which she worked herself' (24 December 1832); but eventually a note of reserve intrudes: 'At 3 we went over to Aunt Sophia's (all our carpets being taken up), to receive the Duc de Nemours. Aunt Sophia of course was *not* present. . . .' (1 September 1835).

The intrigues of Conroy had the effect of creating two rival factions within the royal family. The Duchess professed it her duty to keep Victoria from contact with the King's brood of illegitimate Fitzclarences. William IV, a bluff, eccentric but fundamentally honest man, distrusted the Duchess but wished to see more of his niece and heir-apparent. It was in Conroy's interest to resist these moves and to build up the Princess and her Kensington entourage as a power in the realm. In April 1833 he was to be seen with his wife and daughter escorting Victoria on a ride through the streets of Kensington. He arranged a series of semi-regal tours throughout the country for Victoria and her mother; he also attempted to compel the Princess, when convalescent after an attack of typhoid in 1835, to promise that she would take him as her private secretary after she became Queen. The fact that she had the strength to refuse the demand is a measure of her loathing of Conroy, and of her own will-power at sixteen. She had only Lehzen to support her in this stand for independence; she still felt the absence of the father she had never known; 'It was yesterday *15 years* that it pleased God to take my *most beloved* Papa from us. Alas!' (24 January 1835). But the visit of her cousin Albert of Saxe-Coburg to Kensington in 1836 opened new vistas for the growing girl. Albert was so handsome, so 'full of goodness and sweetness, and very clever and intelligent'. A way of escape appeared at the end of the dark tunnel of Kensington intrigue.

The quarrel with the King came to a head in August 1836. The Duchess of Kent and her daughter then went to Windsor to celebrate his birthday, an invitation impossible to ignore. Before he himself travelled down to Windsor, the King decided to inspect Kensington Palace, where he was apparently horrified to discover that the Duchess had taken over most of the first-floor State Apartments and had partitioned the King's Gallery into three separate rooms. Victoria had recorded the change in a diary entry written after her return from Ramsgate the previous January: 'We instantly went upstairs, that is to say, up *two* staircases, to our new sleeping and sitting apartments which are very lofty and handsome. . . . Our bedroom is very large and lofty, and is very nicely furnished, then comes a little room for the maid, and a dressing-room for Mamma; then comes the old gallery which is partitioned into 3 large, lofty, fine and cheerful rooms. One only of these (the one near Mamma's dressing-room) is ready furnished; it is my sitting-room and is *very* prettily furnished indeed. . . .'

Incensed by what (according to Greville) he pronounced to be the Duchess's appropriation, contrary to his wishes, of 'seventeen rooms', the King launched a bitter attack at his birthday dinner on his sister-in-law – 'the person now near me, who is surrounded by evil advisers' – and formally rebuked her for keeping the Princess from court. Charles Greville's account of the incident has been relied on by numerous historians; it purports to give long verbatim extracts from the speech, but they are based on the recollections of Lord Adolphus Fitzclarence a month after the event. In justice to the Duchess of Kent, it is clear that her daughter's move to a higher floor had been made on medical advice, and that she had obtained the King's permission to use most of the State Apartments on the first floor of the Palace as early as July 1832.

The Office of Works Papers* record a succession of improvements sanctioned at Kensington. In 1828 the Palace was lit by gas, and in 1829 permission was given for an expenditure of £138 for a six-stall shed for the Duchess of Kent's stable establishment. A plan of the first floor, dated July 1832, and signed by Sir Jeffry Wyatville, shows 'the Apartments which His Majesty most graciously allowed to be given up to Her Royal Highness the Duchess of Kent'. These consisted of the King's Gallery, State Dressing Room, State Bed Room, Presence Chamber, Privy Chamber, and the Queen's Drawing Room. She was also allowed to retain the Council Chamber and a small room adjacent to it, which she already had. It was noted, moreover, that the Cupola Room and Great Drawing Room 'may remain open for communication'. By this arrangement the Duchess was granted virtual freedom of the State Apartments; but there was a proviso: 'His Majesty was pleased to observe that in appropriating these Apartments it would be proper to retain their present arrangements and character, in the event of future use.' Most of the rooms in the northern range of Queen Mary's apartments were, incidentally, set aside for storing pictures.

On 7 August 1832, Wyatville submitted an estimate of £7,150 'for repairing, painting and altering various apartments, making a new Kitchen and other Offices, &c., &c.'.

*P.R.O. 19 – 16/1: 121–45. The Royal Archives at Windsor throw no light on the episode of the 'seventeen rooms'.

This included 'the converting the present Chapel into apartments as necessary for Her Royal Highness', but did not include the cost of making a new chapel out of the kitchen offices and turning another department into a laundry, which was estimated at a further £2,000. Wyatville observed that the Duchess had given up the idea of 'dividing the King's Gallery in the State Apartments and sundry other matters, in order to reduce the expence and time that would be required'.

The conversion of the old chapel and the construction of the new was carried out in 1834; a 'Sympathetic Stove' was installed in the new chapel in 1835, but, proving unsympathetic, had to be repaired in the following year. It is possible that all the rooms, old and new, occupied by the Duchess in 1836, may have amounted to seventeen; it is equally obvious that the impression given by Greville's report, that this was a sudden 'take-over' by the Duchess, is misleading. The whole business remains mysterious. Although conceivably the King had rescinded his permission between 1832 and 1836, a more likely explanation may be that his fury was primarily directed at the partitioning of the King's Gallery against his express wishes. He was justified in assuming that the Duchess had abandoned this project; it was certainly an act of vandalism (and, in fact, the partitions were removed and the gallery restored in 1898).

What really lay behind the King's outburst? His latest biographer, W. Gore Allen, has no doubts: 'At a time when, from supposed fear of moral infection, she was keeping Victoria away from the chastest court in Europe, she herself was living in more or less open sin with her chamberlain, Sir John Conroy. William might have overlooked her stupidity; but her hypocrisy was more than he could stomach.'

But was the Duchess of Kent's relationship with Conroy adulterous? The gossiping Greville assiduously propagated the idea, but Lady Longford has marshalled a series of arguments against it – among them, the Duchess's genuine moral principles, the fact that Queen Victoria later denied the imputation, and the wording of the Duchess's own comment in 1854 on 'the death of this man, who has been for MANY, MANY years with me . . . and who has been of great use to me, but unfortunately has also done great harm!'

If 'men of the world' like Lord Melbourne and the Duke of Wellington were prepared to think the worst of the Duchess, Conroy's insolent familiarity with women may have been the cause. But the sexual aspects of his liaisons were probably not his main concern. He sought personal influence and financial gain. When Princess Sophia died in 1848, she was found to have left only £1,600, though her savings must have been enormous; while after Conroy's death £60,000 belonging to the Duchess of Kent was not accounted for.

Victoria's eighteenth birthday, 24 May 1837, was an anniversary that King William had seriously in mind, for he had set his heart on living until she became legally of age to succeed him. On that day his messenger Lord Conyngham delivered a letter from him into Victoria's own hands at Kensington. Conroy and the Duchess tried to intercept it, but failed. In the letter the King offered her £10,000 a year of her own entirely free from her mother's control, an independent Privy Purse, and the right to appoint her own ladies. Conroy and the Duchess were furious. Victoria noted: 'Felt very miserable & agitated. Did not go down to dinner.'

By the next morning, Conroy had concocted a reply for her to sign, in which she was made gratefully to accept the £10,000 but modestly to decline the other privileges and the suggestion that the money should be free from parental control. Though she tried to amend the draft and to consult the Prime Minister, Lord Melbourne, she was compelled to sign. She dictated to Lehzen a statement that the draft was not her own. The King was not deceived: 'The real point,' he commented, 'is the Duchess and King John want money.'

Henceforth Victoria's eyes were fully opened; she steadfastly resisted all attempts to coerce her; often she stayed in her room with Lehzen, and took her meals there. She would not speak to her mother. When Lord Liverpool made a friendly intervention, she told him that she would do without a private secretary altogether, and refused even to consider making Conroy Keeper of the Privy Purse. As the King's life ebbed away, Victoria won the trial of strength. It was a triumph of character.

It is not surprising that she should once have told Melbourne: 'I don't believe Ma ever really loved me.' Time softened her hardness, and years later, after her mother's death, she was filled with remorse when, on reading her private papers, she found overwhelming evidence of her love. Conroy she never forgave. And as for Princess Sophia – there is a legend that her spinning-wheel can still be heard at Kensington Palace; such ghostly labours would be sufficient punishment for this lonely unfortunate spinster.

10 · QUEEN VICTORIA'S ACCESSION

The twentieth of June 1837 is (like 24 May 1819) a day for which Kensington Palace will always be remembered. At twelve minutes past two in the morning King William IV died at Windsor, and the Archbishop of Canterbury (William Howley), the Lord Chamberlain (Lord Conyngham) and the King's physician immediately set out for Kensington. There were delays before they could be admitted and before the Duchess consented to wake 'the dear Child with a kiss', but at six o'clock she was led down the back stairs in her dressing-gown to a sitting-room, which she entered alone. After Lord Conyngham had announced the news, he knelt; she gave him her hand to kiss. Returning to her bedroom, she put on the plain black dress which can at present be seen at the London Museum in Kensington Palace (during storage in the Second World War it turned brown).

At half past eleven the Queen descended to the 'Red Saloon', now the entrance hall of the London Museum, to hold her first Privy Council. The 'Hire of Furniture, preparing for a Council, &c.' went down at £22 10s. od. in the Lord Chamberlain's Accounts. The room was crowded, and the scene has been immortalized by Sir David Wilkie, not entirely accurately, for the Queen is shown as wearing white. The Councillors were struck by the self-possession with which she read her declaration in a clear voice, and by the modesty with which she went through the ceremony of swearing-in. That she approached her old uncle, the Duke of Sussex, rather than allow him to come to her, was a gesture approvingly noticed. All in all, her good nature and sincerity made a favourable impression that even the cynical Charles Greville acknowledged.

It was a busy day, during which the Queen received several dignitaries; wrote to her 'Dearest, Most Beloved Uncle', King Leopold; dismissed Conroy from her Household (though not, of course, from her mother's); and appointed Baroness Lehzen Lady Attendant on the Queen. At nine in the evening she saw her Prime Minister, Lord Melbourne, for the second time within a few hours. She saw him alone, as she did the other visitors, and 'as I shall *always* do all my Ministers'. In the course of the day her bed was taken out of her mother's room, and that night she slept alone for the first time. She wrote in her journal: 'Since it has pleased Providence to place me in this station, I shall do my utmost to fulfil my duty towards my country; I am very young and perhaps in many, though not in all things, inexperienced, but I am sure, that very few have more real good will and more real desire to do what is fit and right than I have.'

The Queen's confidence was immeasurably strengthened by her association with Melbourne, whom she summed up immediately as 'a very straightforward, honest, clever and good man'. Melbourne had charm, an attribute in men to which the Queen always responded, and he approached his duties as her adviser with the right mixture of paternal affection and human sympathy. To a young girl seeking reassurance he could bring a wealth of political experience and philosophical detachment, much useful information, and a carefree wit in conversation that had miraculously survived a tragically disappointing private life. Victoria was enthralled; and she was fortunate in her counsellor. It is amusing to see how often she drew him out about his visits to Holland House and its redoubtable hostess, who as a divorcée could not be received at court. His chief fault was a counterpart of his *insouciance*, that he tended to minimize difficulties, to distrust social change – and this was soon shown in his attitude to Conroy, who had made exorbitant conditions for his retirement from the Duchess of Kent's service, including a pension, the Grand Cross of the Bath, a peerage and a seat on the Privy Council. Conroy's demands were unacceptable, but Melbourne advised that he should be granted a pension and a baronetcy. The weak compromise made Conroy more impossible than ever and brought his retirement no nearer.

These were the last weeks of Victoria's life at Kensington. On 21 June she held another Privy Council at St James's, less fully attended than the first, and on 27 June she received addresses from the House of Commons at Kensington Palace. On Thursday, 13 July, she recorded her departure in her diary:

'Got up at 8. At ½ p. 9 we breakfasted. It was the *last time* that I slept in this poor old Palace, as I go into Buckingham Palace today. Though I rejoice to *go* into B.P. for many reasons, it is not without feelings of regret that I shall bid adieu *for ever* (that is to say *for ever* as a DWELLING), to this my birth-place, where I have been born and bred, and to which I am really attached! I have seen my dear sister* married here, I have seen many of my dear relations here, I have had pleasant balls and *delicious* concerts here, my present rooms upstairs are really very pleasant, comfortable and pretty, and *enfin* I like this poor Palace. I have held my first Council here too! I have gone through painful and disagreeable scenes here, 'tis true, but still I am fond of the poor old Palace . . . the poor rooms look so sad and deserted, everything being taken away. . . .'

Running through these lines one notices – apart from the fourfold repetition of the word 'poor', a Teutonic habit she never lost – a deep affection for her early home. It is in fact largely owing to Queen Victoria that the buildings of

*Princess Feodore of Hohenlohe, her half-sister, who was married when Victoria was nine.

Kensington Palace still stand intact. But some of her affection also went to Kensington as a place, the little village that was already being lost in speculative building. After a drive to Windsor a few weeks later, the Queen wrote: 'All along the road the people were very loyal and civil, and my poor native place, Kensington, particularly so. . . .' The banner with the word VICTORIA that had been hoisted over Kensington Palace on her eighteenth birthday reflected the sentiment of the natives as much as Conroy's ostentation. The contemporary public house in the Earls Court Road, the Princess Victoria, still stands as evidence of local loyalty.

The Queen thoroughly enjoyed the first year of her reign, which culminated in her coronation in June 1838, a day that she recognized as 'the *proudest* of my life' until the day of the opening of the Great Exhibition eclipsed it. She put her new-found affluence to immediate use by beginning to pay off her father's debts. It was typical of Conroy that he should have explained the Duchess of Kent's financial difficulties by saying that she had paid off those debts already, which was quite untrue. The Queen also royally demonstrated her gratitude for loyal service, and her long memory, by creating Mr Sotherton Peckham-Micklethwait a baronet because he had held down one of her horses' heads in a carriage accident at Hastings in 1833 – perhaps an excessive reward.

Her second year as Queen was less happy. She soon encountered criticism, first in the scandal of Lady Flora Hastings, next in the larger crisis of her Ladies of the Bedchamber. When Lady Flora, one of the Duchess's unmarried ladies, was suspected of being pregnant, the Queen too readily jumped to the conclusion that Conroy was responsible; in fact, Lady Flora was not pregnant – she was suffering from a tumour on the liver from which she soon afterwards died. The public scandal which was aroused and the tragedy in which it culminated taught the Queen a sharp lesson, not to judge by appearances; it is unlikely that she would have made this error if it had not been for the feud persisting between her mother's household and her own.

The suspicions and hatred engendered by the Hastings affair were revived when Lord Melbourne went out of office, and Sir Robert Peel requested the Queen to make some changes in her ladies, who were predominantly Whig. The Queen flatly refused; eventually she had her way, and the choice of her ladies was never again allowed to become a political issue; but sixty years later the Queen admitted that youth and inexperience had led her to stand too firmly on her dignity.

The long-delayed resignation of Conroy from the Duchess's household in June 1839, after pressure from the Duke of Wellington, brought welcome relief to the Queen and opened the way to reconciliation with her mother. A second visit from her cousin Albert the following October renewed her dreams of a happier future. Such 'beautiful blue eyes', such an 'exquisite nose', 'such a pretty mouth with delicate moustachios and slight but very slight whiskers' were altogether too much. It was a pleasure just to look at Albert 'when he gallops and valses'. On 15 October she delicately staged her proposal of marriage; and Albert 'said he would be very happy *das Leben mit Dir zuzubringen* . . .'.

In the short space of two years Victoria had cut herself free from a sordid tangle of intrigue. At a very early age – and not without setbacks – she had asserted her rights and independence in the face of more difficulties than most of us encounter in a lifetime. She was not yet twenty-one, but the Kensington child had indeed become a woman.

11 · QUEEN MARY'S BIRTHPLACE

Although Queen Victoria rarely visited Kensington Palace after her accession, the Palace was often in her mind and its future became a source of anxiety to her. The rooms were now fully occupied, so far as funds were available for repairs. It is largely owing to the Queen's personal interest that the buildings survived intact into the twentieth century.

The upkeep of this and other Crown property was to prove an increasing financial problem throughout her reign. As early as 1838, Lord Duncannon, the First Commissioner of Woods and Forests, proposed to Lord Melbourne that they might 'take down the bad part of Kensington Palace, which does not interfere with the better part of the Palace'. (RA. Z. 501/18). The suggestion was shelved.

The Queen returned to Kensington on 19 June 1848: '. . . In the afternoon, at 5, I drove with Flora McDonald to Kensington Palace, in order to see the very unique and curious collection of Pce. Wallenstein's pictures of Byzantine and old German schools. Albert and Mr Gruner met me there. There are 101 pictures all most beautifully finished. The sight of my old rooms brought back so many recollections, the gardens too, – just the same. . . .' (RA. Queen Victoria's Journal, 19 June 1848.) After Prince Albert's death, she sent his 'collection of early pictures, at Kensington Palace', to the National Gallery. (9 January 1863. RA. Vic. Add. P.P. 1591.)

In 1852 the Queen appointed Mrs Lyons, wife of the Inspector of Buckingham Palace, to be housekeeper at Kensington Palace, in place of her predecessor Mrs Dale, who had died. (RA. F. 38/13.) She had no intention of losing the accommodation which the Palace afforded, but meanwhile she had to answer a proposal that the Palace should be used for a new National Gallery. This she countered in a masterly memorandum to Lord John Russell of 5 March 1851, which has been published in Volume II of the Benson and Esher edition of her Letters:

'The Queen would give every facility to the selection of a good site for a new National Gallery, and would therefore not object to its being built on to Kensington Palace or anywhere in Kensington Gardens; but does not see why it should exactly be placed upon the site of the present Palace, if not for the purpose of taking from the Crown the last available set of apartments. She is not disposed to trust in the disposition of Parliament or the public to give her an equivalent for these apartments from time to time when emergencies arise. The surrender of Kensington Palace will most likely not be thanked for at the moment, and any new demand in consequence of such surrender would be met with lavish abuse. As to economy in the construction, it will most likely be best consulted by building on a spot perfectly free and unencumbered.'

By 13 March her resolution had hardened, and in approving the committee appointed to consider a site, she added the proviso: 'on the understanding that any site in Kensington Gardens except the Palace was open to their choice'. (RA. C. 9/92.)

The threat to the Palace continued, nevertheless, and in June 1856 Prince Albert wrote to Lord John Russell:

'I hear that the Bill for the site of the New National Gallery is to be violently contested & that Ld. Elcho hopes to gather a sufficient number of votes for his "Times" proposal to take Kensington Palace from the Crown for the purpose & to throw away the site which we have acquired. It will be very important that the Members of the Commission of 1851 should stand up boldly for

H

their own recommendation which has been arrived at after much deliberation & towards the realization of which 5 years labour & £350,000 have been spent! . . .' (RA. F. 26/30.)

The decision to proceed with the National Gallery plans was a great relief. On 18 June 1860 the Queen again went to Kensington: '. . . In the afternoon, which was oppressive, drove with Alice & Horatia S. to Kensington Palace and visited Ly. C. Barrington in her apartment, which is exceedingly pretty. . . . Walked in the small private garden I knew so well and looked up at the windows of my old rooms, now so deserted, & which contain the whole history of my childhood! . . .' (RA. Queen Victoria's Journal, 18 June 1860.) But the Queen continued to be worried at the uneasy relationship between the Board of Works and the Crown and the Sovereign. In October 1860 the case of a lodge at Bushey Park led her to write another memorandum to her Prime Minister:

'. . . In the instance referred to, a lodge, upon the death of its occupier, was claimed by the widow to whom the Queen had promised the same upon her husband's decease. The Commissioner of Works reports however that the lodge is to be pulled down, under a minute of the Treasury, on the recommendation of a former local inspector. – On enquiry it appears that this transaction has been completed entirely without the Queen's knowledge, and she is sorry to have to observe that this is by no means a solitary instance of buildings belonging to the Crown, and even sometimes in occupation of the Sovereign, being, by an understanding between the Board of Works and the Treasury, allowed to fall out of repair, with a view of afterwards pulling them down, as beyond the reach of repair. The Queen may refer to Kensington Palace and Kew Palace, the future fate of which give Her some anxiety.

It is evident that if this practice be continued, the Crown will in time lose all its buildings, not actually inhabited, and if the principle be recognized any of its Palaces might be condemned without the least knowledge of the Sovereign, or available remedy. . . .'

The Queen went on to argue that the Sovereign and Parliament had the legal duties of any life-tenant of property, not to allow it to deteriorate, and she asked for an annual survey of the royal buildings. (RA. A. 28/153.) Her firmness seems to have removed any immediate threat to Kensington Palace.

Some idea of the use to which the Queen would have liked to put her apartments at Kensington can be gathered from a correspondence in March and April 1861 between Florence Nightingale's brother-in-law Sir Harry Verney and Sir Charles Phipps, Keeper of the Queen's Purse. Sir Harry was anxious to obtain a quiet apartment for Miss Nightingale, who was living in an hotel but still hard at work, though in poor health. Phipps told Sir Harry Verney that it would give the Queen 'sincere pleasure' to offer any accommodation or assistance in her power to Miss Nightingale 'in the glorious mission to which she has devoted herself'. Enquiries were actively pursued to see whether the Kensington apartment of Princess Sophia, who had died in 1848, could be repaired for her. Prince Albert was sure, said Phipps, that the House of Commons would vote the necessary sum, 'if they knew that the apartment was to be given to Miss Nightingale, who has worked so hard for the good of others, & never before asked or received anything for Herself'. Verney told Phipps that Miss Nightingale did not need many rooms: only a good-sized, quiet sitting-room, 'and it is very desirable that the bedroom should be quiet overhead'.

The restoration of Princess Sophia's quarters seems to have been agreed upon in principle, until it was found that large-scale rebuilding would be necessary. On that note the correspondence ended, and Kensington Palace lost the opportunity of receiving a distinguished resident. It is doubtful whether Florence Nightingale ever knew of Sir Harry Verney's application. (R.A. Vic P.P. 7353.)

In April 1867 Prince Franz of Teck (who became a Duke of Württemberg in 1871) and his newly married wife, the former Princess Mary Adelaide of Cambridge, a cousin of Queen Victoria, moved into the apartment at Kensington Palace in which the Queen had been born (Plate XI). To be exact, they took over, in Princess Mary Adelaide's words, 'the greater portion of the apartment' that the Queen and 'Aunt Kent' had occupied; and they were very pleased to receive this 'very charming abode, as the rooms are handsome and comfortable'. To finance the move, they borrowed £8,000 from Miss Coutts.

Princess Mary Adelaide was a good-looking, generous, delightfully high-spirited woman. Unfortunately she was extremely large. It was, no doubt, her bulk which had kept her unmarried until the age of thirty-three. The Prince of Teck was four years her junior, attractive in looks, highly strung (and increasingly frustrated), and as dark as she was fair (an attribute that in itself recommended him to Queen Victoria who was morbidly aware of the dangers of lymphatic blood). The couple lived to no great age, the Duchess dying in 1897 and the Duke in 1900.

However, this is to anticipate. They had gone into the Palace, as the Duke and Duchess of Kent had done in 1819, in preparation for the birth of their first child. Again the child, born on 26 May 1867, was a girl destined for a glorious future. Kensington Palace has always been associated with women – and Queens – of remarkable character; but it was a strange coincidence that Queen Mary, who strikingly resembled Queen Victoria in steadfastness and dignity, should have been born in the same house two days after the Queen's birthday. The coincidence was not lost on Queen Victoria – and it was accentuated by the fact that the little girl (her god-daughter) was given the names Victoria Mary, though she was to be known as 'Princess May' until her marriage to Prince George in 1893.

Her warm-hearted mother ('Fat Mary') was a popular figure with Londoners; a large crowd gathered round Kensington Palace on the morning after the birth of her daughter. Queen Victoria sent her a quilt which she had helped to work, and in June she drove to the Palace to see mother and child in the bedroom in which she had formerly slept with her own mother; she found 'a *very* fine child, with quantities of hair – brushed up into a curl on the top of its head! – & very pretty features & a dark skin' (Plate XI). According to precedent, Kensington signalled its acceptance of its new residents by naming another public-house in the Earls Court Road – this time the Prince of Teck.

Princess May was the first of four children; the other three were boys. She inherited her father's interest in art and furniture and his talent for 'interior decoration'. It meant much to her to have been born in the Palace, which stimulated her sense of history, her love of the past and of royal relics.

The Tecks lived luxuriously, giving dinner-parties in the ground-floor Council Room. Princess May took an interest in the guests, and her exceptional memory enabled her to preserve recollections of them. Of the generation of her grand-mother, the Duchess of Cambridge (who lived until 1889), only one other survivor remained since the death of the Duchess of Kent in 1861; she was the Duchess of Inverness, second wife of the Duke of Sussex, a neighbour of the Tecks at Kensington Palace until she died in 1873. Dispensing hospitality in a dining-room 'fitted up like a tent', she made generous presents to the Teck children. The Duke of Sussex's retired page, Mr Beckham, could also be visited in his little house (probably Temple Lodge) near the Serpentine. Queen Victoria and the children remembered each other's birthdays; Princess May sent her a plate painted by herself, and she collaborated with her brothers in a handkerchief case which (she wrote) 'we lay most respectfully at Your feet'.

The Tecks' life at Kensington, with its incessant hospi-talities, soon put them into debt with the local tradesmen. Cheerfully vague about her finances, the Duchess made a celebrated speech when opening a new church hall at Kensing-ton, to which Mr John Barker, the grocer, had contributed. 'And now I must propose a special vote of thanks to Mr Barker,' she said with unconscious candour, 'to whom we all owe so much.'

But Kensington was not to be a permanent home for Princess May. The Round Pond was still thought to be dangerous, and at fourteen months she had an illness, either 'a slight chill, or the effluvia from the pond in Kensington Gardens, which was in a very unhealthy state, and which the nursery windows face', said her mother. Such reflections contributed to the Duchess's wish to acquire a second home. The Kensington apartments were maintained, but by 1870 the Tecks were also settled at White Lodge, Richmond Park – a step reluctantly approved by Queen Victoria, who knew that they could not afford to run two homes. At Richmond the Duke of Teck occupied himself with gardening and changing the furniture. The children grew strong, but Princess May was rather shy and silent, perhaps because her mother talked so much. Taglioni's dancing lessons, sometimes held at Kensington Palace, became a trial for her.

Princess May's chief childhood companions, beside her own brothers, were the Prince of Wales's children; she also paid visits to the homes of her German relations at Rumpenheim, Neu Strelitz and Reinthal. But throughout her childhood a financial crisis was building up for her parents. The debt to Miss Coutts increased to £50,000, and by 1882 £18,000 was owed to tradespeople. After endless family discussions, and in return for embarrassing loans, it was decided that Kensington Palace must be given up and that the Tecks, like other royal predecessors who had lived not wisely but too well, must go into temporary exile. Thus in 1883 Princess May and her parents departed for a stay of two years in Florence, which naturally increased her love of the arts. She never lived at Kensington again, though, like Queen Victoria, she never forgot her birthplace.

12 · RESTORATION OF THE PALACE

Queen Victoria acquired another link with Kensington Palace when her sixth child, Princess Louise (Plate XII), went to live there in 1873 after her marriage to the Marquess of Lorne; she occupied the rooms left vacant by the death of the Duchess of Inverness, and she continued to reside at the Palace until her own death in 1939. Princess Louise was a 'slow developer' with something of an inferiority complex, but early showed artistic talent. As time went on, the Queen saw her as 'a clever, dear girl'. She championed her unconventional engagement to one of her subjects, and used all her tact to ease a difficult situation when the couple became estranged in 1880, after Louise had sustained severe injuries in an accident while Lord Lorne was Governor-General of Canada. The Queen visited her on 10 March 1875:

'Drove with Beatrice and Janie C. to Kensington, getting out in the inner Court at the Palace, and Louise took me upstairs to her sitting-room, where I had never been, and showed me her other rooms, which are very nicely arranged. Amongst her spare ones, are my old bedroom & the little room attached to it. Though quite unfurnished, when I went in & saw the well known look out, the doors, etc. where I had spent 16 years of my life everything came back again so vividly to my mind. There I had slept with dear Mama till 35 when Sir J. Clark wished us to go up still higher into the rooms now belonging to Mary (Duchess of Teck). These old rooms were Mama's but were given back to Uncle Sussex, when Mama & I left Kensington in 37. Downstairs Louise has several rooms opening into each other & a fine Drawingroom. The Diningroom is also nice, but a great deal has still to be furnished, & the long corridor to be cleaned. Left again a little before 6. . . .' (RA. Queen Victoria's Journal, 10 March 1875.)

On the same day she wrote emotionally to her daughter about the sight of her former bedroom – '& then *downstairs* the old rooms where so *many* lived – including dear Papa! A *whole* world of recollections streamed back! – I loved the old Home – tho' it often was not a very gay or even happy one! And I am happy to think one of my daughters shd. live in a part of it. . . .' (RA. Vic Add MSS. A/17. 625.)

On returning from Canada in 1883, Princess Louise and her husband occupied rooms in the south-west corner of the Palace; the Princess had a studio in their walled garden. It was here that she worked on the impressive statue of her mother which now stands on the Broad Walk, and is the gift of the Queen's 'loyal subjects of Kensington'. The Queen travelled up from Windsor for its unveiling on 28 June 1893:

'My Coronation Day. . . . At ½ p. 4, started with Beatrice, Liko* & Marie L. for London, the Equerries & 4 Ladies in attendance, the other Gentlemen having gone on before. Got out at the Addison Rd. Station & drove in an open landau with 4 horses to Kensington. My old native town was beautifully decorated, though, unfortunately just when we were in the middle of the High Street, a most violent storm, almost like a waterspout came on & we had to shut the carriage. We drove up the Broad Walk to the spot opposite the front of Kensington Palace where stood the statue which was to be unveiled, the statue of me in my Coronation robes, done by Louise, & erected by the inhabitants of Kensington in memory of my Jubilee. Several tents were put up, all the members of my family, & a great number of people were present, & there was a Guard of Honour & a Band. Almost directly after I arrived, the rain ceased & I was able to have the

*Prince Henry of Battenberg, Princess Beatrice's husband.

carriage opened. Sir A. Borthwick M.P. for Kensington read a very nice address, to which I answered the following: "I thank you sincerely for this loyal address, & for the kind wish to commemorate my Jubilee by the erection of a statue of myself on the spot where I was born & lived till my accession. It is a great pleasure to me to be here on this occasion in my dear old Home, & to witness the unveiling of this fine statue so admirably designed & executed by my beloved Daughter." Mr Glyn, the Vicar, read an address from the parishioners of Westminster. Bertie* performed the unveiling ceremony, after which Lorne presented a number of gentlemen to me. The statue stands beautifully with its back to the private garden of the Palace & facing the Round Pond. Took tea with Louise and Lorne before coming back & got home at 7.' (RA. Queen Victoria's Journal, 28 June 1893).

The Queen had given her short speech considerable thought. There are two drafts of it in her handwriting in the Royal Archives at Windsor.

The subject of Kensington Palace usually occurs in the Royal Archives when retainers or their dependants are petitioning for rooms; or when those fortunate enough to have obtained them are complaining about the state of the decoration (such as Miss Harriet Phipps in 1874, whose 'drawing-room paper is peeling off the wall'. RA. Vic. P.P. 16706). But as she grew older, the Queen lived increasingly in her Kensington past, and her memory approached total recall. Asked by the *Graphic* in 1895 to approve a picture of the scene when she received news of her accession, she dictated the following comments: 'Lord Conyngham who is kneeling should not have a grey coat but a black one. His hair was a

*The Prince of Wales.

very dark not reddish. The Archbishop should not have a Cloak on but the usual dress of a Bishop. . . .' (RA. Vic. P.P. 11609.)

She was now 76, and Kensington Palace was still not entirely safe. But during the closing years of her reign she made an arrangement with Lord Salisbury, the Prime Minister, and Sir Michael Hicks-Beach, the Chancellor of the Exchequer, by which she undertook to give up Bushey House and the Ranger's House at Greenwich on the understanding that the Government should purchase and place at her disposal Schomberg House, and should restore Kensington Palace. Parliament voted £23,000 for this purpose, on condition that the State Rooms should be opened to the public.

The Times commented on the decision with approval on 28 January 1898, and pointed out that the upper part of the house; the 'Denmark Wing' (Queen Mary's Gallery); and the Orangery had been allowed to get into an appalling state. There was much to be done, but fortunately, said *The Times*, most of the ceilings were watertight, though there were bad holes in the main staircase. Workmen were already engaged on the floors, as several joists had rotted away; however, the structure was basically sound. *The Times* rejoiced that the lath-and-plaster partitions in the King's Gallery, which divided it into three rooms with shabby grates and mantelpieces, would be swept away to show the Gallery in its original glory. Outside, potting-sheds and frames filled the area between the Palace and the Orangery, which had itself been grievously damaged, and its oak panelling torn down. All this would now be tidied up, and the Orangery carefully restored. *The Times* mentioned that it had been seriously proposed to pull down the whole Palace, and that 'Her Majesty's subjects ought to be grateful to her for having strenuously resisted such an act of Vandalism'.

The success of the restoration was largely due to Reginald

Brett, Secretary of the Board of Works. Mr Ernest Law has described the work in his guide-book of 1899, the rebuilding of walls, reslating of roofs, cleaning of ceilings. The oak wainscoting of the Queen's Staircase (or Denmark Staircase) was 'as black as your hat'. The looking-glasses over the chimney-pieces in Queen Mary's Gallery, made by Gerard Johnson and Robert Streeter in 1690, were 'literally dropping to pieces'. Kent's ceiling in the King's Drawing Room was so dirty as to be nearly black. As for the Grand Staircase (Plate V): 'No one who did not see this staircase before the restorations were begun,' wrote Law, 'can conceive the woeful state of dust, filth, decay and rot which it then presented. With the fine iron balusters broken, damp oozing from the walls, the paintings indistinguishable from incrustations of smoke, and strips of the painted canvas hanging from the walls in shreds – it seemed impossible that it could ever be restored to its pristine splendour.'

Law's guide (1899) lists 278 pictures as hanging in the restored State Apartments. This figure may be compared with Faulkner's list (1820) of more than 600 works (excluding wall and ceiling paintings) formerly in the Palace, which was based on a catalogue made in 1818 by Benjamin West. In 1700 the Palace had housed the best part of the royal collection, but some of the finest pictures had subsequently been removed to Windsor or Buckingham Palace. Most of the canvases described by Faulkner were removed in the first half of the nineteenth century to Hampton Court. As late as 30 September 1838 a charge of £2 4s. 3d. was included in the Lord Chamberlain's Accounts for 'Removing Pictures to Hampton Court Palace.'* Some of the pictures were returned to Kensington from Hampton Court in 1898; among the few originally at Kensington and now to be seen at the Palace are the portraits in King William's Gallery of Katherine Elliot by John Riley

*Public Record Office.

and J. B. Closterman, and of the philosopher Robert Boyle by Johann Kerseboom, and in Queen Mary's Gallery the portrait by Kneller of Peter the Great, who visited William III at Kensington Palace.

The display of pictures arranged in 1898, and brought to Kensington from various royal residences, was selected primarily for historical interest in this context rather than for artistic merit. Law's guide names a number of pictures painted by Benjamin West for George III, and he is still strongly represented in the current collection. Queen Victoria's nursery and bedroom were decorated for the reopening with prints and momentoes of her reign; but the rooms have been subsequently rearranged, with great skill and taste, by the late Queen Mary.

The State Rooms were opened to the public on the Queen's eightieth birthday, 24 May 1899. Ten days earlier, she made her own private inspection (Plate XIII):

'. . . Left Windsor for London at $\frac{1}{2}$ p. 11. Drove with Beatrice, Ducky* & Ernie† direct from Paddington to Kensington Palace, where we got out at my old entrance. I was carried up the state staircase & went through a number of rooms I had never seen before, including some very fine ones in what is called the Denmark Wing, where Pce. George of Denmark lived. These rooms have been restored & put into good order. Pictures of my life & reign have been hung, also some good ones from Hampton Court. The rooms are to be thrown open to the public, as it is thought they would be of great interest, but on the condition that they may be taken back at any time for the use of my family. I also went down to the lower floor, into the two large rooms, in the first of which I held my First Council, & then also into the one in which I was born. This used to be used as Mama's writing room & then as a visitor's room. Mr Brett met us at Kensington, &

*Princess Victoria Melita of Edinburgh.
†Ernest Louis, Grand Duke of Hesse, 'Ducky's' husband.

explained everything. He has the merit of the whole arrangement. . . .' (RA. Queen Victoria's Journal, 15 May 1899.)

Sir Arthur Bigge (later Lord Stamfordham) accompanied the Queen on her tour of the Palace and described it as 'a most interesting and in many ways a touching experience'. He mentioned that the Queen was doubtful about the identity of the room in which she was born, and that 'when we got into the "Cupola Room" the Queen said she had never seen it before —!' (RA. L 5/108.) The fact that the Queen failed to remember many of the State Apartments seems to be an additional argument against William IV's contention that the Duchess of Kent had effectively appropriated 'seventeen rooms'.

This was the Queen's last visit to her birthplace, a fitting close to her long and loyal association with Kensington. In December 1900 the Duke of Argyll (formerly Lord Lorne) and Princess Louise were hosts at a luncheon in the Palace to Canadian soldiers home from South Africa; and at the end of the year following Queen Victoria's death in January 1901 Kensington became a Royal Borough, as she had wished.

13 · BARRIE'S KENSINGTON GARDENS

> 'Where *Kensington* high o'er the neighb'ring lands
> 'Midst greens and sweets, a Regal fabrick, stands,
> And sees each spring, luxuriant in her bowers,
> A snow of blossoms, and a wilde of flowers,
> The Dames of *Britain* oft in crowds repair
> To gravel walks, and unpolluted air.
> Here, while the Town in damps and darkness lies,
> They breathe in sun-shine, and see azure skies;
> Each walk, with robes of various dyes bespread,
> Seems from afar a moving Tulip-bed,
> Where rich Brocades and glossy Damasks glow,
> And Chints, the rival of the show'ry Bow. . . .'

These are the opening lines of a long poem published in 1722 by Thomas Tickell. The title was *Kensington Garden*, not, be it noted, 'Kensington Gardens', which at that time were still in embryo. In fact, Tickell's poem centred around the sunken garden to the north of the Palace, devised by Henry Wise out of a gravel-pit and praised by Addison. The fanciful Tickell saw this hollow as the site of 'the proud Palace of the Elfin King' and declared that it was 'far far sweeter in its ancient days'. He made up a fairy story about the princeling Albion who fell in love with the beautiful Kenna ('that gave the neighb'ring town its name') and was slain by his rival Azuriel, who lived farther to the west, 'where now the skies high *Holland-House* invades'. He saw the royal gardener as re-creating the ancient fairy city:

> 'The walls and streets in rowes of yew designs,
> And forms the Town in all it's ancient lines.'

It was a laboured poem, but Tickell seems to have been the first to establish a fairy mythology for Kensington, which was reasserted more confidently by Barrie in Edwardian days.

Matthew Arnold's 'Lines Written in Kensington Gardens' (1852) may also have held inspiration for Barrie. Arnold invoked the 'red-boled pine-trees' and the 'tremulous sheep-cries', but the hint that Barrie followed appeared perhaps in the later verses:

'In the huge world, which roars hard by,
Be others happy if they can!
But in my helpless cradle I
Was breathed on by the rural Pan.

Calm soul of all things! make it mine
To feel, amid the city's jar,
That there abides a peace of thine,
Man did not make, and cannot mar.'

Kensington Gardens have received glancing references from many other writers, from Sheridan, who objected that the birds' 'ridiculous chirruping ruins the scene . . . and gives me the spleen', to Crabbe and Arthur Symons, who declared 'Love and the Spring and Kensington Gardens, Hey for the heart's delight!' But the history of the Gardens, as sketched in *The Times* throughout the nineteenth century, is a long series of public complaints and grievances. The ravages of disease in the elms alongside the Broad Walk were deplored many years before they had to be cut down in 1953, to be replaced by oak and copper beech. The intention of building on land west of the Palace was denounced in the correspondence columns in 1838 and 1840, but failed to prevent the rise of Kensington Palace Gardens in the forties and fifties; it was the death blow to J. C. Loudon's pet scheme to extend the Gardens to Holland Park by way of Campden Hill. Two other losses in the

Queen Victoria arriving to inspect restoration work on her last
visit to Kensington Palace, 15th May, 1899 (see p. 107).

(see p. 107).

PLATE XIII

Clock Court, Kensington Palace (*Crown Copyright*).

PLATE XIV   'An afternoon when the gardens were white with snow'.
Drawing by Arthur Rackham for *Peter Pan in Kensington Gardens*, 1906
(see p. 114).

nineteenth century were 'King Henry VIII's Conduit', demolished in 1871, the oldest building in Kensington, designed to supply Chelsea Palace with water, and Vanbrugh's Water Tower, built to provide water for Kensington Palace; both stood on Palace Green.

In 1843 the creation of the Flower Walk was welcomed in *The Times*. In the fifties and sixties band-playing on Sundays received praise, criticism, and ultimate acceptance; the concerts brought large crowds to the Gardens. More generally deprecated by *Times* correspondents was the behaviour of small boys who robbed birds'-nests, destroyed plants and caused alarm by throwing stones at the chestnuts. Nurse-maids flirting with the soldiery were disapproved in 1858; the stench of mud cleared from the Round Pond provoked the letter-writers in 1886.

By the middle of the nineteenth century the Gardens had become very popular. A census of persons entering them on Sunday, 26 August 1855, shows a total of 61,458. (RA. Add. Q/221.)

It was not until the turn of the century, however, that Kensington Gardens made their chief contribution to literary history and acquired a lasting mythology from J. M. Barrie. He was then forty, living at 133 Gloucester Road, married but without children of his own, and perhaps with some thwarted sense of paternity. Like Lewis Carroll, he had a great love of children and a gift for devising games for them. Unlike Carroll, he was more concerned with boys than girls; the former made friends with Dean Liddell's daughters, the latter with the sons of Arthur Llewelyn Davies and his wife Sylvia, daughter of George du Maurier. Barrie met the boys in Kensington

Gardens; he played with them there, at their Kensington home, at his little house in Gloucester Road, and at his country house, Black Lake Cottage, near Farnham. His big St Bernard dog Porthos, a constant companion, became the original of Nana in *Peter Pan*. In 1902 Barrie moved to Leinster Corner in Bayswater Road; his walks with the Davies boys in the Gardens continued.

The first fruit of their adventures, inspired by games of pirates and Red Indians at Black Lake Cottage, was *The Boy Castaways of Black Lake Island* (privately printed, 1901). But the inspiration of Kensington Gardens proved more important. It resulted in that formless, rambling book *The Little White Bird* (1902), which introduced Peter Pan into the world. In its pages is to be found the germ of many of Barrie's plays, but particularly of *Peter Pan*, produced at the Duke of York's Theatre on 27 December 1904; and the great success of the play led to the publication of *Peter Pan in Kensington Gardens* (1906), which consisted of the six chapters from *The Little White Bird* that concern Peter Pan. The text is slight, but, being adorned with delightful colour plates by a rising illustrator, Arthur Rackham, it made a handsome gift-book for Edwardians young and old. The collaboration between Barrie and Rackham invested the scenes of Kensington Gardens with an imaginative glow which still clings to them.

Fairies flourished in the years of material prosperity before 1914; they have been out of fashion since. But whether or not Barrie's fancies should be deprecated for archness and sentimentality need not be argued here (the present writer, having had to play Tinkerbell to his parents' Pan and Wendy, has his views on that point). What is certain is that Barrie had the genius to ensure Peter Pan's survival and to link him with Kensington Gardens. Since 1912 he has been commemorated by George Frampton's statue on the southern bank of the Serpentine, which was placed at the point where Peter Pan first landed from his boat. In 1928 the statue was tarred-and-feathered, and in 1952 Peter Pan's pipes were stolen, being subsequently recovered in Staffordshire by a sharp-eyed policeman.

The Gardens contain a miscellaneous collection of statuary, but Peter Pan and Queen Victoria are the only subjects who are properly indigenous. Since 1893 the Queen has been seated with dignity before the eastern front of the Palace. Since 1876 Prince Albert ('The Gold King') has been seated under the canopy of the Albert Memorial – which is as much a symbol of the age as the story of the curate's egg; but he belongs to the Albert Hall and to the great museums on the other side of the road, rather than to Kensington Gardens. Watts's 'Physical Energy'; Edward Jenner, in his chair at the head of the Serpentine; and the obelisk to the explorer J. H. Speke, were even more chancy acquisitions.

Kensington Gardens remain what they were in Barrie's day, unrivalled airing and exercising ground for children of the upper classes. They are used by all ranks and ages, but their location has ensured that they should be visited most by the children of the well-to-do and their nurses. For children it is a unique, exciting place; Barrie gave a child's-eye view of it – and of Queen Victoria. 'She was the most celebrated baby of the Gardens, and lived in the palace all alone, with ever so many dolls, so people rang the bell, and up she got out of her bed, though it was past six o'clock, and she lighted a candle and opened the door in her nighty, and then they all cried with great rejoicings, "Hail, Queen of England!" ' As a historian Barrie would have been even more deplorable than Dickens.

When he describes the boats on the Round Pond, his touch

is happier. 'There are men who sail boats on the Round Pond, such big boats that they bring them in barrows, and sometimes in perambulators, and then the baby has to walk. The bow-legged children in the Gardens are those who had to walk too soon because their father needed the perambulator.' The failure of Porthos to scare the town sheep in the Gardens is also well observed: 'He cannot with dignity retreat, but he stops and looks about him as if lost in admiration of the scenery, and presently he strolls away with a fine indifference and a glint at me from the corner of his eye.'

Barrie and Rackham show us 'the Hump, which is the part of the Broad Walk where all the big races are run', St Govor's Well (now a drinking-fountain), the Flower Walk (which he calls 'Baby Walk'), the Gardens under snow (Plate XIV), and the island in the Serpentine. But of course it is 'after Lock-Out Time' that the Gardens, and with them Peter Pan and the fairies, come to life. And peering through the railings in the darkness, we may still wonder.

14 · THE TWENTIETH CENTURY

After the death of Queen Victoria, the Duchess of York (later Queen Mary) assumed, to some extent, her role of guardian angel of Kensington Palace. Her association with her birthplace had been much shorter than that of Queen Victoria, but an acute historical sense made her just as keenly aware of its interest and value, while her enthusiasm as a collector recalled that of George II's Queen, Caroline of Anspach (a comparison that she accepted). Perhaps she communicated her views to her husband, King George V, for according to Lord Esher, writing in 1912, 'King George's dream, and no one knows better its visionary character, is to pull down Buckingham Palace, to round off St James's and the Green Parks at Constitution Hill and Buckingham Gate, and then, with the money obtained by the sale of the Gardens of Buckingham Palace, to reconstruct Kensington Palace as the town residence of the Sovereign.' A dream indeed, but one made fascinating by the identity of the dreamer.

Meanwhile, work at the Palace continued throughout Edward VII's reign, with a view to making more of the Palace and of its domestic gardens available to the public. In 1907 the King's Privy Chamber (the Council Chamber) was added to the rooms that could be visited. In May 1909 visitors were able to admire the transformation in the ground to the north-east of the Palace that had been planned ten years earlier. The potting sheds between the Palace and the restored Orangery had now been swept away, and a new entrance devised by means of a gravel path from the Broad Walk leading to the porch of Queen Mary's Staircase. A most attractive innovation was the sunken garden with its lily pond and flower beds.

The project for a London Museum took shape during the reign of Edward VII. He gave the idea his personal encouragement. It owed initial impetus to C. E. Jerningham, whose valuable collection of prints and engravings of the Royal Parks and Palaces of London was accepted by the King in 1906 on behalf of the nation. King Edward frequently visited his sister Princess Louise of Kensington, but he paid a special visit to the Palace to see the Jerningham collection in 1906, and it was then exhibited in the renovated Council Chamber.

The Museum was eventually established at Kensington in 1911 by the second Viscount Esher and the first Viscount Harcourt, with the warm approval of George V and Queen Mary. A large number of objects representing the life and history of London were displayed, mostly in the State Apartments, under the direction of Guy Laking, the first Keeper and Secretary. Many royal relics were put on show, including the wedding dresses of Queen Mary and her mother, which joined such relics as Queen Victoria's dolls' house, which had been in the Palace since her childhood.

Still more typical of the later attractions of the London Museum, however, was an annexe housed in the stable buildings and entered by a door nearly opposite the Orangery. Here visitors could see several of those panoramic models of Old London which have always especially appealed to children. There was also a Roman galley, and a number of relics of a more grisly description – a prison cell from Stepney, a condemned cell, an execution axe, thumb screws, leg irons, 'hand crushers', and so forth.

The London Museum did not stay long at Kensington Palace. In 1913 Lord Leverhulme presented Stafford House (renamed Lancaster House) to the nation, so that the collections could be more fittingly exhibited there. Lancaster House made a splendid home for the museum until 1945; subsequently, as we shall see, it again returned to Kensington Palace.

With the death of Queen Victoria, her daughters acquired a sharp change of status; they became the King's sisters. One who particularly felt the change was Princess Beatrice (Plate XII), the youngest child. As a girl she had been her mother's constant companion; after the death of the Queen's indispensable attendant John Brown in 1883, the burden had become still heavier. Her wish to marry Prince Henry of Battenberg ('Liko') distressed the Queen, and was gratified only on the understanding that they should live with her. Accordingly, after their marriage in 1885, they had settled into a suite of rooms at Windsor Castle.

Many years earlier, 'Liko's' cousin, the Grand Duke of Hesse-Darmstadt, had married the Queen's second daughter Princess Alice. She had died young in 1878, and in 1884 their daughter Victoria had married her cousin, 'Liko's' elder brother Prince Louis of Battenberg; they were the grandparents of the Duke of Edinburgh.

Fortunately, the Queen grew very fond of 'Liko' and of the four children born to him and Beatrice between 1886 and 1891. The young family spent most of their time at Windsor, Balmoral and Osborne, and the parents often travelled with the Queen; Princess Beatrice continued to receive confidences that were denied to her brother 'Bertie', the Prince of Wales. 'Liko's' death from malaria in 1896, while serving with the Ashanti expedition, came as a great grief not only to his widow but also to the Queen. Afterwards Princess Beatrice

stayed with her mother to the last; during the Jubilee cele-
brations of 1897 she rarely left her side.

Princess Beatrice had long been associated with the Isle of
Wight; she had been married at Whippingham Church, and
had become Governor of the Island; now Osborne Cottage,
left to her in her mother's will, became her principal home;
but she soon acquired an apartment at Kensington Palace,
where she had a neighbour in her sister Princess Louise. In
1917 her sister-in-law the Duchess of Albany left Claremont
and moved into Clock House on the north side of Clock Court;
and henceforth the Duchess's daughter (Princess Beatrice's
niece) Princess Alice, Countess of Athlone, has resided at the
Palace, where she still lives (1968). The Palace therefore
remained 'functional' and continued to hold an important
place in the affections of the royal family.

In 1905 Princess Beatrice gave a ball at Kensington Palace
for her eldest daughter Victoria Eugénie (Ena), aged eighteen.
Princess Ena, an attractive, popular girl, became a centre of
fashionable interest and speculation in Edwardian days.
Soon after the ball, she got engaged to King Alfonso of Spain,
whom she met at a dinner in Buckingham Palace. They were
married in Madrid in May, 1906, and very nearly lost their
lives immediately afterwards, when a bomb was thrown at the
royal coach, killing two of the horses.

Queen Ena often stayed at Kensington with her mother.
Her last visit as Queen of Spain was in 1931. In January of
that year Princess Beatrice slipped on a mat at Kensington
Palace and fell heavily, breaking two bones in her left arm.
Her condition was complicated by bronchial trouble; she
became so seriously ill that her daughter hurried from Madrid
and stayed with her for a month. Queen Ena returned to
Madrid in some trepidation as to the reception she would
receive, for Spain was then threatened by revolution. In fact,
she was warmly welcomed; but in April a swing to Republican-

ism in the Spanish elections compelled King Alfonso and his Queen to leave the country.

During the First World War King George V placed a number of rooms in Kensington Palace at the disposal of those who were working for Irish prisoners-of-war and Irish soldiers at the front; several thousand parcels were sent off each week, a task in which Queen Mary and the Princess Royal took an interest. A small part of the Gardens was used for allotments or occupied by the military; but the greater part was more than ever appreciated by those seeking rest and recreation. The vast camp established after the war for troops taking part in the Peace Parade caused a more serious disturbance. In July 1919 Kensington Gardens looked like Salisbury Plain, being crowded with soldiers from all over the world, grey Italian uniforms mingling with blue French tunics, the scarlet tassels and headdress of French marines, and Indian turbans. The task of catering for their individual tastes in food was enormous; huge marquees were set up.

The State Apartments at the Palace were closed in 1913, partly owing to the risk of damage by suffragettes, and remained closed throughout the war, and for some time afterwards. Reopened in 1923, they attracted many visitors at first, but when the crowds dwindled it was decided to limit the public days to Saturday and Sunday from April to November. In 1933 Queen Victoria's Bedroom, in which Queen Mary had been born, and the two adjoining rooms were refurnished and redecorated under the direction of Queen Mary, who assembled from Frogmore, Buckingham Palace and elsewhere, objects associated with Queen Victoria or characteristic of her reign. Wall-paper was printed from old blocks of the period, and items from Queen Mary's own collection of furniture and pictures were later placed in these rooms. Outside, in Kensington Gardens, a graceful bandstand between the Round Pond and the Flower Walk, and a new refreshment room near the Serpentine were successful innovations during the thirties.

15 · THE SECOND WORLD
WAR AND AFTER

Kensington Palace, like London in general, suffered much more severely from the Second World War than from the First, though after an initial closure the State Apartments were reopened in May 1940. The damage was of two kinds: from occupation by the military, and from enemy bombing. In 1940 King George VI allowed the Army to use the rooms on the south side of Clock Court, which became the headquarters of No. 34 Personnel Section: a patriotic decision that had to be paid for long afterwards when these apartments were restored for residential occupation.

Air-raid damage to the Palace by incendiary bombs was announced on 4 November 1940. The worst raids were on 14 and 15 October; four separate fires were soon brought under control, and valuable pictures were saved from the State Apartments; the homes of Princess Beatrice in the east wing and of Princess Alice in Clock Court were affected, but the injury to the north and east sides of Prince of Wales's Court proved the more serious in the long run because it was never thoroughly repaired. Some of the State Apartments showed signs of damage when they were reopened in the summer of 1942, and later the effects of a flying-bomb explosion compelled their closure until 1949. But on the whole the Palace, covering, as it does, several acres, escaped lightly.

Nevertheless, the bombing caused great inconvenience to some residents at the Palace. After leaving Canada, where her husband the Earl of Athlone had been Governor-General, Princess Alice returned to Kensington in 1946 to find their apartments still uninhabitable owing to the damage of fire and water. In *For my Grandchildren,* she has written:

'Our apartments there were in complete chaos. The disastrous fire had destroyed part of our roof and attic rooms, though even greater damage had been avoided by the torrents of water that had deluged the whole place, and the house had remained un-repaired since 1940. No window frames were left and all our furniture, books and pictures were heaped higgledy-piggledy in the drawing and dining rooms. In these circumstances, kind Aunt May [Queen Mary] kept us with her until our home was restored to some sort of order. As everywhere else, help was unprocurable. . . . Aunt May even came to help wash china. . . .'

Princess Louise, Duchess of Argyll, was spared the sight of the bomb damage – and of the military occupation of her own residence which followed her death. Her life at the Palace had always been simple and unconstrained, a reaction to the strict formality of her mother's gatherings, where she had felt disgraced by such an innocent expression as a sneeze. Sympathy for children was instinctive; one mother had told her that her daughter was worried about her ability to curtsy in her presence; the Princess rushed across the room as soon as she saw the girl, picked her up, kissed her, and said: 'Did you remember to bob, dear?'

She died at Kensington Palace on 3 December 1939, aged ninety-one. The news made its impact even in wartime, for the Princess was held in affection far outside the royal family. Her body was cremated at Golders Green before the funeral at Windsor, which was attended by the King and Queen and many royal mourners. The art of Princess Louise is less well known than it deserves, particularly her oils and water-colours which she did not feel able, in her position, to exhibit or sell, except occasionally for charity. But as a talented sculptor she will be remembered for her Kensington statue of Queen Victoria and for her bronze memorial in St Paul's to the men of the Dominions who died in the Boer War.

Princess Beatrice, the last survivor of Queen Victoria's children, lived until the age of eighty-seven. If the disfavour into which the German name Battenberg fell in the 1914–18 war was temporarily disturbing, the death in action of her son Prince Maurice in 1914, aged twenty-three, and the loss in 1922 of another son, Lord Leopold Mountbatten, after an emergency operation at Kensington Palace, had been terrible blows; Lord Leopold was only thirty-three. And her own later years were much troubled by rheumatism; she was compelled to use a wheel-chair, and to have doors made in Queen Victoria's Council Room (at present the entrance hall of the London Museum), so that she could go into the gardens. She suffered from cataract and was nearly blind before an operation improved her sight. After this, she could no longer read music – a deprivation for one who had once composed a march for the Grenadier Guards. But she was able to complete her very valuable editorial work on her mother's papers, for which she was uniquely qualified, and in 1941 she published selections from the diary of her great-grandmother, which she had chosen and translated.

The compensations of age included the company of her great-nephew Prince Philip (later the Duke of Edinburgh), who often stayed as a boy at Kensington Palace with his grandmother, the Dowager Marchioness of Milford Haven, mother of Earl Mountbatten of Burma. The Marchioness occupied the apartment at the north-west corner of Prince of Wales's Court.

The young Victoria had been told that 'Uncle Sussex' would punish her if she was naughty. It is said that Prince Philip was warned not to blow his toy trumpet too loudly, as it might disturb Princess Beatrice; but unless he took his trumpet into the Palace garden, it would have needed a powerful blast to reach his great-aunt, for the apartments are some distance apart.

Princess Beatrice died on 26 October 1944, at Brantridge Park, Balcombe, Sussex, the country home of the Earl of Athlone and Princess Alice. Her recently widowed daughter Queen Ena had reached her side the day before. She was buried at Windsor, but after the war her body was transferred to the chapel in Whippingham Church, where she rests beside her husband.

A sale of Princess Beatrice's furniture, silver, pictures, and books was held at the Palace over three days in April 1946. Her surviving son, the Marquess of Carisbrooke, lived at No. 10, Kensington Palace, from 1956 until his death in 1960.

The Palace had come through the Second World War more or less intact, at least as regards those portions which are now open to the public. Kensington Gardens also remained essentially the same, and in 1945 a proposal to erect temporary bungalows there was resisted; but, as after the previous war, the Gardens were disturbed by preparations for the Victory Parade in June 1946. Miles of barbed wire were used to enclose a camping site for troops, and latrines and wash-houses with corrugated iron roofs were erected. There were huts between the Orangery and the Bayswater Road for German prisoners of war working on the camp.

The historian of these years finds little to record. The wedding of Prince Philip and Princess Elizabeth (later Queen Elizabeth II) in 1947 brought Kensington Palace momentarily into the news, for Prince Philip spent the night before the ceremony at the apartment of his grandmother the Dowager Marchioness of Milford Haven. In 1950 the Marchioness died, when her residence in the north wing appropriately came into the possession of Princess Mary of Cambridge, Duchess of

Beaufort, daughter of Prince Adolphus of Teck ('Prince Dolly') and grand-daughter of Princess Mary Adelaide; her husband is Master of the Horse to Queen Elizabeth II. An exhibition of the restored Rubens paintings from the Banqueting Hall in Whitehall was held in the Orangery in 1950.

Meanwhile, a decision taken by King George VI had affected the future of the Palace for at least fifteen years. It had become clear that Lancaster House would continue to be reserved for international conferences, as it had been for several years, and that the London Museum must again seek a new home. Accordingly, in 1950 King George VI granted to the Trustees for fifteen years the use of part of Kensington Palace as temporary accommodation, and in July 1951 the London Museum was reopened to the public in the rooms below the State Apartments where its collections were first exhibited. In May 1952, in the last year of her life, Queen Mary paid a visit to the Palace to study the details of Queen Victoria's Coronation robes, which she felt should form a precedent for those of Queen Elizabeth II.

More than twenty rooms on the ground floor (including the room in which Queen Victoria was born) and in the semi-basement of the main building, on the site of the original Nottingham House, have since been occupied by the Museum; and many visitors have not only enjoyed the fascinating historical exhibits, models, costumes, children's toys and royal and theatrical relics, but have also been led to take an interest in the Palace itself, and to explore the State Apartments above, which have been open free daily in summer and winter and administered by the Museum since 1956, after redecoration and re-arrangement. In November 1956 Queen Elizabeth visited the State Apartments to see some of Queen Mary's possessions which had been placed there.

In many ways Kensington Palace, with its individual charm and remarkable historical associations, makes an ideal home for the London Museum. The atmosphere is propitious and the arrangement has had many advantages; but unfortunately the space available is insufficient to display more than a small proportion of the numerous treasures the Museum has acquired. In 1959 the Standing Commission on Museums and Galleries reported that the Museum was much too cramped in its rooms at Kensington, and in 1961 the Common Council of the City of London approved in principle a scheme to amalgamate the London Museum with the Guildhall Museum and to house the combined museums in a new building near Aldersgate Street in the City.

The proposal was criticized in letters to *The Times* in July 1961, which pointed out that the London Museum was pleasantly withdrawn from the overcrowded city, that it made good use of an historic building, and that its limited display had the advantage of sparing visitors the exhaustion common to museums. These considerations were outweighed in the eyes of the Trustees by the difficulties of storing so many of its possessions, and, among other things, by the lack of parking facilities around the Palace. The decision was therefore taken to move to the modern building in the City; but many obstacles have arisen, including serious delays on the building site, and the increase of costs, originally estimated at £1,500,000. Sometime, no doubt, the London Museum will leave Kensington – when its departure will revive the problem of the future maintenance of the Palace – but that time is not yet.

After £17,000 had been spent on the State Apartments by 1949, and after the re-establishment of the London Museum,

A general view from the air of Kensington Palace, Kensington Gardens, Hyde Park, and St. James's Park (see p. xvii).

Kensington Palace from the air (see p. xvii).

PLATE XV

Princesses' Court, Kensington Palace
(*Crown Copyright*) (see pp. 35–6).

PLATE XVI — Staircase in the apartment of Princess Marina, Duchess of Kent, at Kensington Palace, showing portrait of the Duke of Kent, father of Queen Victoria (see p. 127).

which cost £50,000, the Ministry of Works began the enormous task of arresting the decay in other parts of the Palace. The most immediate object was the restoration of Princess Louise's apartment in the south-west wing as a residence for Princess Marina, Duchess of Kent. These rooms were in a terrible state of repair, and £127,000 was allotted for the work, which began in November 1952. Sir David (later Lord) Eccles had to answer questions in the House of Commons about the extent of the estimate (December 1953). He said that the entire Palace had been sadly neglected by the previous government, and declared that it was misleading to consider expenditure in terms of one particular 'house'; the restoration of a Palace of outstanding historic and architectural interest was a duty. A new boiler-house was now installed to serve the whole Palace, including the London Museum, at an estimated cost of £42,000.

Expenditure on this scale emphasized that the difficulty of preserving the Palace as a national monument in a deteriorating economy had greatly advanced since the Victorian years; and ever-rising costs meant that estimates, already large, tended to grow from month to month. Nevertheless, it was a satisfaction to lovers of Kensington Palace to read, on 21 October 1955, the first Court Circular to come from the Palace for many years, giving details of an engagement of the Duchess of Kent. Since then her apartment (Plate XVI) has been Princess Marina's principal residence; her children, Prince Edward Duke of Kent and Princess Alexandra, also lived there until their marriages, while Prince Michael still does so.

The use of the Palace by members of the royal family was extended after the marriage of Princess Margaret, Countess of Snowdon, and Lord Snowdon in 1960. During the first years of their married life they lived in the delightful panelled rooms of the Maids of Honour, No. 10 Kensington Palace, in the north wing, which had become vacant on the death of the

Marquess of Carisbrooke. But they soon required larger accommodation for their growing family, which was offered to them in the rooms on the south side of Clock Court that had formerly been occupied by the Duke of Sussex. In 1961 and 1962 protests were raised in the House of Commons at the expenditure involved. In the House, on 4 April 1962, Lord John Hope stated that defective plaster, rotting timber and some vaulting were being removed, but that the rest of the structure, including internal brickwork, windows, roof-stack and Wren staircase, was being left and made good. Later in the year, in response to further questions, it was emphasized that part of the expense was being met by Princess Margaret herself. Certainly, no one with knowledge of the cost of maintaining and restoring old property could suppose that any extravagance was involved.

The history of the Palace ends, as it began, with a fire on the south side of Clock Court. The fire broke out in January 1963 in the roof above the servants' quarters of Princess Marina's residence. Seventy firemen with ten pumps answered the call. The damage caused further delay in completing the work on Princess Margaret's apartments next door. This fire was fortunately not so serious as that which had alarmed Queen Mary in 1691, but it was bad enough; it was watched by Princess Marina, Princess Alexandra, Prince Michael and Princess Margaret with some natural apprehension.

It is pleasant to be able to take leave of Kensington Palace while it still serves a useful purpose as the home of members of the royal family, of their children, and of former or active servants of the Queen and her relatives. The Palace has been the seat of five monarchs and has been at the centre of great affairs of state. It has suffered long periods of neglect and the threat of demolition, but the turns of fortune have always retrieved it for good use; it has sheltered the eccentric and unfortunate as well as the dignified and dedicated; its State Apartments have become one of the sights of London, its grounds a famous park; it has housed a great museum. John Thorpe would have been astonished to know what was in store for the modest house that started life on his drawing-board.

The happy accident that the Palace was Queen Victoria's birthplace not only enhanced its historic interest but greatly helped to ensure its survival. As the birthplace of Queen Mary it acquired another ardent defender. Very noticeable, indeed, is the association of the Palace with women of character. From Queen Mary II, joint sovereign with William III, Queen Anne, Queen Caroline of Anspach, Queen Victoria, Princess Louise, to Queen Mary, Princess Marina and Princess Margaret in our own day, one is aware of a strain of unusual and persistent determination, mingled with gifts of art and talent, and of a continuing affection for 'this poor old Palace'. All the womanly qualities of intuition and practical management have been abundantly demonstrated within these walls. Mary II's affection for 'Dutch William', Queen Anne's conflict with the Duchess of Marlborough, Queen Caroline's handling of her straying husband, Queen Victoria's youthful struggle with Sir John Conroy – each can be studied at length elsewhere, but all are united by their Kensington setting.

Kensington Palace is thus an unusually human place. Its unpretentious domesticity strikes the visitor at once. He is aware of the applied pomp of the Cupola Room and the King's Staircase, but, like the Palace itself, he shrugs them off as inessential and a trifle absurd – a point that Kent seems to be making in his staircase paintings. Looking out from the windows of the State Apartments to the Round Pond and the distant vista to the Serpentine, he is still left with the impression – accurate, as it happens – of a gentleman's country house unexpectedly caught up in grand affairs.

This sense of personal intimacy makes Kensington Palace unique among our royal residences. It does not insist; it offers refreshment, suggests a quiet contemplation of three hundred years of history. Fortunate in its champions hitherto, the Palace more than ever needs sympathetic understanding if its fabric is to be kept intact in the straitened circumstances of modern Britain.

BIBLIOGRAPHY

Alice, H.R.H. Princess, *For my Grandchildren* (1966).

Allen, W. Gore, *King William IV* (1960).

Anon, *An Essay towards the Character of Her late Majesty Caroline, etc.* (1738).

Anon, *Kensington Palace: An Illustrated Guide to the State Apartments* (1958).

Anon, *Royal Commission on Historical Monuments* (*England*). Vol. II. London West (1925).

Anon, *The London Museum: An Illustrated Guide* (1960).

Arkell, R. L., *Caroline of Anspach: George the Second's Queen* (1939).

Ashley, Maurice, *The Glorious Revolution of 1688* (1966).

Aspinall, A. (Ed.), *The Later Correspondence of George III.* Vol. III (1967).

Beattie, John M., *The English Court in the Reign of George I* (1967).

Benson, A. C. and Esher, Viscount (Eds.), *The Letters of Queen Victoria: A Selection from Her Majesty's Correspondence between the years 1837 and 1861.* 3 vols (1907).

Bolton, Arthur T. and Hendry, H. Duncan (Eds.), *The Wren Society, Vol. VII* (1930).

Braybrooke, Neville, *London Green* (1959).

Chapman, Hester W, *Mary II Queen of England* (1953).

Chettle, G. H. and Faulkner, Patrick A, 'Kensington Palace and Sir Christopher Wren: A Vindication'. *Journal of the British Archaeological Association.* Third Series, Vol. XIV (1951).

Curtis Brown, Beatrice (Ed.), *The Letters and Diplomatic Instructions of Queen Anne* (1935).

Darlington, W. A., *J. M. Barrie* (1938).

Davies, J. D. Griffith, *A King in Toils* (George II) (1938).

Defoe, Daniel, *A Tour Thro' the Whole Island of Great Britain* (1724–7; new edition, 1927).

Duff, David, *Edward of Kent* (1938). *The Life Story of H.R.H. Princess Louise Duchess of Argyll* (1940). *The Shy Princess* (Princess Beatrice) (1958).

Esher, Viscount (Ed.), *The Girlhood of Queen Victoria: A Selection from Her Majesty's Diaries between the years 1832 and 1840.* 2 vols. (1912).

Faulkner, Patrick A., 'Nottingham House: John Thorpe and his Relation to Kensington Palace'. *Archaeological Journal.* Vol. CVII (1952).

Faulkner, Thomas, *History and Antiquities of Kensington* (1820).

Fulford, Roger, *Royal Dukes* (1933).

Gaunt, William, *Kensington* (1958).

Gleichen, Lord Edward, *London's Open-air Statuary* (1928).

Green, David, *Gardener to Queen Anne* (1956). *Sarah Duchess of Marlborough* (1967).

Greville, Charles, *The Greville Memoirs.* Ed. Lytton Strachey and Roger Fulford. 8 vols. (1938).

Hervey, John, Lord, *Some Materials towards Memoirs of the Reign of King George II.* 3 vols. (1931).

Hopkinson, M. R., *Anne of England* (1934).

Hunt, Leigh, *The Old Court Suburb* (1860 edition).

Hussey, Christopher, 'Kensington Palace'; *Country Life,* 29 November, 6 December, 13 December (1924). 'Kensington Palace: The Apartments of the Countess Granville'; *Country Life,* 1 September 1928.

Imbert-Terry, Sir H. M., *A Constitutional King: George the First* (1927).

Law, Ernest, *Kensington Palace: The Birthplace of the Queen* (1899); revised to include London Museum exhibits (1912).

Loftie, W. J., *Kensington Picturesque and Historical* (1888). *Kensington Palace* (1898).

Longford, Elizabeth, *Victoria R.I* (1964).

Millais, J. G., *Life and Letters of Sir John Everett Millais,* Vol. I (1900).

Neale, Rev. Erskine, *Life of His Royal Highness Edward Duke of Kent* (1850).

Ogg, David, *William III* (1956).

Oman, Charles, *A History of England* (1895).

Pope-Hennessy, James, *London Fabric* (1939). *Queen Mary 1867–1953* (1959).

Pyne, W. H., *History of Royal Residences, etc.,* Vol. II (1819).

Rait, R. S. (Ed.), *Royal Palaces of England* (1911).

Robb, Nesca A., *William of Orange: A Personal Portrait* (Vol. I, 1962; Vol II, 1966).

Rutton, W. L., 'The Making of the Serpentine'. *The Home Counties Magazine,* Vol. V (1903).

Summerson, John (Ed.), *The Book of Architecture of John Thorpe in Sir John Soane's Museum.* Walpole Society, Vol. 40 (1966).

Tisdall, E. E. P., *The Wanton Queen* (Queen Caroline of Brunswick) (1939).

Trevelyan, G. M., *History of England* (1926). *England under Queen Anne.* 3 vols. (1930–4).

Walpole, Horace, *Memoirs of the Reign of George the Second.* Vols. I–III (1847). *Letters,* Vols. I–III, Ed. Peter Cunningham (1857). *Memoirs and Portraits,* Ed. Matthew Hodgart (1963).

Waterson, Nellie M., *Mary II, Queen of England* (1928).

Weaver, Sir Lawrence, *Sir Christopher Wren: Scientist, Scholar and Architect* (1923).

Woodham-Smith, Cecil, *Florence Nightingale 1820–1910* (1950).

The Royal Archives, Windsor Castle; the Public Record Office; the collection of the Kensington Public Library; the library of the London Museum; *The Dictionary of National Biography;* and the files of *The Times* have been consulted.

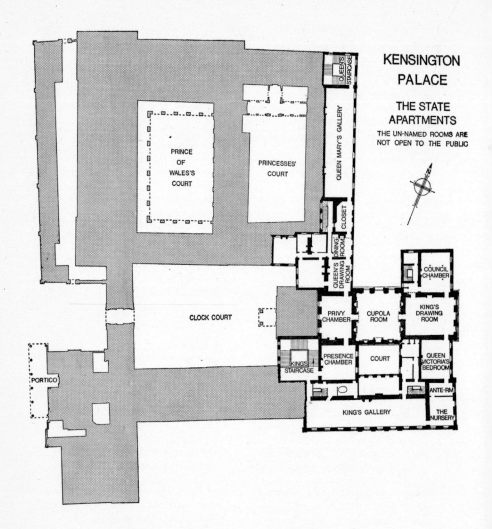

KENSINGTON
PALACE

THE STATE
APARTMENTS

THE UN-NAMED ROOMS ARE
NOT OPEN TO THE PUBLIC

QUEEN'S STAIRCASE

QUEEN MARY'S GALLERY

PRINCE
OF
WALES'S
COURT

PRINCESSES'
COURT

CLOSET

N

QUEEN'S DINING DRAWING ROOM

COUNCIL
CHAMBER

CLOCK COURT

PRIVY
CHAMBER

CUPOLA
ROOM

KING'S
DRAWING
ROOM

KING'S
STAIRCASE

PRESENCE
CHAMBER

COURT

QUEEN
VICTORIA'S
BEDROOM

PORTICO

ANTE-RM

KING'S GALLERY

THE
NURSERY

BLOCK PLAN
GROUND FLOOR LEVEL
THESE PARTS OF THE PALACE
ARE NOT OPEN TO THE PUBLIC

10 0 10 20 30 40 50 60 70 80 90 100 FEET   5   0   5   10   15   20   25 METRES

Note: The Stone Gallery (referred to, *inter alia,* on p. 67), running between
the portico and the King's Staircase, also the Guard Room, no longer exist
in their original form.

134

INDEX

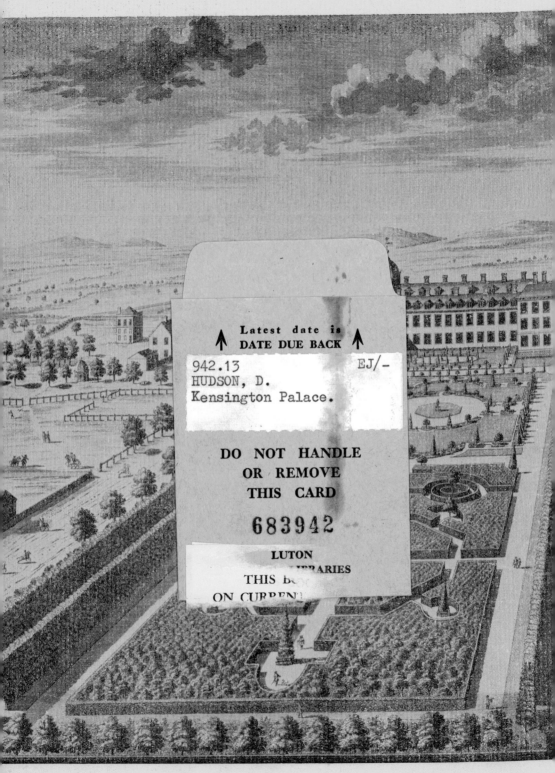

Perspective view of Kensington Palace i